Lap Around the Sun

Lap Around the Sun © Copyright 2025 by William C. Barron All rights reserved.

No portion of this book may be reproduced in any form without written permission from the publisher or author, except as permitted by US copyright law.

ISBN: 979-8-9987695-3-5 (paperback); 979-8-9987695-2-8 (e-book)

Library of Congress Catalog Number:

Cover art in collaboration with Ashely Barron (www.ashleybarronphotography.com)

Editing and Organization in collaboration with Colleen Sell (via Reedsy.com)

First Printing: 2025

29 28 27 26 25 5 4 3 2 1

William C. Barron
Bend, Oregon
simplebender.com

Table of Contents

Introduction 1
January 5
February 38
March 69
April 101
May 133
June 165
July 196
August 229
September 261
October 293
November 326
December 357
About the Author 389
Let's Go Around, Again 390
Index 391

Lap Around the Sun
Daily Steps Forward

William C. Barron

Acknowledgments

Life's lessons surround us — in philosophy, history, and the many diverse traditions of faith and thought. We can all learn, if we are willing to listen. This manuscript would not have been possible without the wisdom of philosophers, teachers, social thinkers, and spiritual guides, both past and present.

I am deeply grateful to my wife, Jan, whose patience, love, and encouragement helped keep me grounded in life's lessons throughout this journey.

My thanks also to my parents, for instilling in me the gifts of critical thinking and acceptance, and to my sons and their families, who continue to broaden my understanding with new perspectives, every day.

Have Courage, Be Bold, and **Never Fear the Dream**

Introduction

In a world increasingly fragmented by competing ideologies and disconnected ways of thinking, *Lap Around the Sun: Daily Steps Forward* offers a unifying journey through humanity's greatest wisdom traditions. This daily companion transcends cultural and philosophical boundaries, weaving together the profound insights of Eastern contemplation, Western rational thought, and African communal wisdom into a harmonious collage of human understanding.

Each day presents a fresh perspective, a new lens through which to view your life and the world around you. The book's title, *Lap Around the Sun*, reflects both its 366-day structure and a more profound truth: that each year of our lives is a precious journey, filled with opportunities for growth, understanding, and transformation. Like the Earth's eternal dance around the sun, the book's wisdom moves in a natural cycle, touching upon essential themes that resonate with the fundamental human experience.

While many books focus on one philosophical tradition, *Lap Around the Sun* offers a unique integration of diverse philosophical traditions. Rather than presenting these wisdom traditions as separate or competing entities, the book reveals their underlying connections and universal truths. You might find a Stoic principle illuminated by an Ubuntu concept, a Taoist teaching enhanced by Judeo-Christian wisdom, or Thomism, Deism, and Nietzscheism ideas. This cross-pollination of ideas creates a richer, more nuanced understanding of life's essential questions.

The book is organized around eight core themes—Amor Fati (embrace (love) fate), Mortality, Emotion, Awareness, Social Thought, Action, Problem Solving, and Resilience—providing a comprehensive framework for personal growth. The principles and philosophies centered around these themes aren't merely theoretical constructs; they are also practical tools for navigating life's challenges and opportunities. The Amor Fati sections teach us to embrace our circumstances rather than fight against them. The Mortality readings help us face life's finite nature with courage and purpose. The Emotion and Awareness sections guide us through the landscape of our inner world, while Social Thought connects us meaningfully with others. The Action, Problem Solving, and Resilience segments provide practical strategies for meeting life's challenges with wisdom and grace.

Each daily contemplation begins with a powerful quote or principle, followed by a thoughtful narrative that unpacks its meaning for contemporary life. These daily reflections serve as bridges, connecting ancient wisdoms to contemporary challenges and philosophical insights to practical actions.

Lap Around the Sun is more than just an inspirational, motivational book. It is a compass for your life's journey and a unique tool for personal transformation and spiritual growth. ... Whether you're a young professional seeking meaning in your career, or a middle-aged adult navigating life transitions, or simply someone hungry for a deeper understanding of yourself and your place in the world.

I approached this project, acknowledging that there are no fixed rules governing our lives, but there are abiding principles that can guide us. In this book, which reflects my interpretation of the relevance and application of these timeless principles to modern life, I've endeavored to respect each reader's individual path while providing the wisdom of countless generations as a guide to create a space for personal discovery within the context of shared human experience.

Although these 366 daily contemplations appear in this book as they were initially written—in chronological order, January 1 through December 31—they can be read in any order you choose.

LAP AROUND THE SUN

You can start by reading a daily contemplation in May or any other month, and randomly skip around to other daily contemplations. Or you can read all contemplations focused on a particular theme, such as Awareness or Problem-solving, one a day or as many a day as you wish. I intend for Lap Around the Sun to be your daily companion, read and re-read as you journey through the different seasons of your life, offering fresh insights and inspiration with each day, helping you find purpose and connection in every precious, unrepeatable moment.

WILLIAM BARRON

January

January 1

Amor Fati

Love fate. Embrace where and what you are experiencing now.

Amor fati is Latin for "love of fate." A keystone of Stoic philosophy, amor fati is the acceptance of where you are and what you are doing, the recognition and facing of the joy, pain, pleasures, and fears of your present situation. At worst, it may be the only way to get through a struggle. At best, you will find something you love and enjoy in every situation. You usually cannot change your circumstances, but you can always change your perspective and attitude—those you control.

Acceptance isn't passivity or surrender. It's stopping the struggle with something you cannot change. Acceptance lets your energy work for you, not you against the unchangeable.

Start fresh each year, each month, each week, each day, each morning. Be ready to create your future. Your Lap Around the Sun starts now, on this day, in this moment.

January 2

Mortality

Engage in the world while you are alive.

In a world filled with noise and chaos, it can be tempting to retreat and bury your head in the sand in a futile attempt to block out the constant static. You might find yourself striving not to engage, not to become entangled in the web of events that unfold around you. However, it is important to realize that your presence and participation in this world are not only necessary but also desired.

This tumultuous world needs you—your ideas, your contributions, and your spirit. Those around you—your family, friends, colleagues, and even strangers—need and want you to be engaged, to be a part of the community. They crave your input and the unique perspective only you can provide.

Find a way to find a way to involve yourself, to immerse yourself in the world around you, and to remain engaged. Life is fleeting, so while you are here, ensure that your legacy is one of active participation and engagement. Strive to stay involved and impact the lives of others. After you are gone, you might still impact lives through the memories you leave and the changes you enact during your lifetime. Your existence is significant, and your involvement can make a world of difference.

January 3

Emotion

Happiness and pleasure, just as sorrow and pain, are part of life. When emotions are intense, unbridled, and/or pervasive, they become obstacles to overcome in pursuit of your self-vision.

Emotions, by nature, tend to be benign but can swing to extremes. Seldom are they just neutral, because they are often perceived as affirmation or negation. If they were consistently neutral, we would not recognize their importance and influence. Yet, uncontrolled or suppressed emotions can become obstacles in our pursuit of enlightenment and spirituality, which we must acknowledge and yet overcome. Emotions are responses—for example, to happiness and sorrow, pleasure and pain, confidence and uncertainty. The more we allow emotions to run uncontrolled, the greater the risk of being controlled by them rather than the inverse. Our emotions can work to our advantage, but we must be aware that they can also be used as weapons against us.

Manage your emotions, and no one can manage you.

January 4

Awareness

The two times we are most vulnerable are when we first begin and when we are at our peak. The first is due to inexperience; the second is due to arrogance.

Inexperience and arrogance have been the downfall of many individuals throughout history.

Inexperience is a state we are all familiar with, a state we are born into. It is a natural part of our journey, but willful or prolonged inexperience can inhibit our growth and advancement. With a concentrated focus we can accumulate experience. Although inexperience can be an obstacle, it can be conquered with hard work and dedication.

Arrogance poses a much more significant challenge. It is an intoxicating and often deceptive state of mind, one that we must first acknowledge and recognize before we can begin to deal with it. Without this recognition, much like any addictive drug, arrogance has the power to consume us, to take over our thoughts and actions, and ultimately, if left unchecked, to destroy us from within.

Therefore, remaining eager to learn, grow, and better yourself and never giving in to complacency or arrogance are crucial to your life. Embrace the wisdom that comes with experience, and never let go of the humility that should come with it.

January 5

Social Thought
People are to be cherished and things used.

In our contemporary society, we often find ourselves asking: Why are we so callous toward life and insatiably covetous of material objects? It is a profound question that demands our attention. People, with their complexities, emotions, and potential for growth, are the essential fabric of our lives; inanimate objects simply are not. Despite the temporary joy or convenience they may bring, material possessions hold no enduring value. They will inevitably break, be stolen, become obsolete, fall from popularity, or lose their value to the possessor.

It is the people and the memories we form with them that impact us the most and stand the test of time, remaining with us forever. These experiences and memories can keep us warm on cold nights, bring smiles to our faces during difficult moments, and remind us of the love we've shared and the lessons we've learned together.

Endeavor to moderate your quest and affection for things. Allocate more time and effort to cherishing the people around you. This includes not only your loved ones and those you may not care for, but also those you may not know personally. Awaiting you will be a greater fulfillment and purpose in your life.

January 6

Action

Thoughts, dreams, and aspirations aren't real—unless and until you put them into action.

We often find ourselves caught up in a whirlwind of wishes, hopes, and dreams, spending our days yearning and striving for a better life, a better world. In our minds, we paint this vivid picture of a world that is starkly different from the reality we live in. We allow ourselves to drift into this dreamlike state, only to be harshly awakened by the stark contrast of our actual circumstances, which can oftentimes feel like a nightmare.

All the time and energy we spend on these thoughts, dreams, and plans are essentially wasted if we do not put them into action.

Only through action can you effectively manifest your dreams into your reality. It is crucial to take hold of your life, seize control of your actions, and begin making tangible, deliberate steps toward achieving your goals and dreams

No one else can do this for you. Others may guide you, assist you, or motivate you, but the ultimate responsibility for transforming your dreams into reality lies with you. You hold the power to build the life and world you've always dreamed of. It all begins with you. It is all up to you.

January 7

Problem Solving

Complex assignments, like life, are just a series of small, discrete, simple, integrated tasks.

Set big, bodacious goals. Study them, organize them, and start accomplishing them in small, discrete, manageable tasks. That is how this book came to be—years of reading and taking notes, organizing my notes and thoughts, and writing, one day at a time, not all at once. Never let any complex problem overwhelm you. Like life itself, every project is an intricate pattern of smaller integrated tasks that you can figure out and accomplish. Do not be overwhelmed by the totality. Focus first on the accomplishable.

January 8

Resilience

Champions understand the fleeting moment of victory. They relish it for what it is and recognize what it is not, then step to the start line for the next race against all comers.

Triumphant arms raised in victory are more fleeting than the painful sting of defeat. Champions, those who have tasted the sweet nectar of success and the bitter pill of failure, have experienced both. They not only thrive on these extremes; they also use them as fuel to grow stronger. They understand that each of these moments, whether of victory or defeat, is nothing but a mirage and exists only for a moment in time. Despite the transient nature of these experiences, champions do not shy away from them. Instead, they sharpen their focus, work tirelessly, and constantly revise their strategies. Regardless of whether they are basking in the glory of winning or nursing the wounds of losing, champions are always eager and always ready. Without fanfare or spectacle, they are prepared to face the next challenge and challengers, ready to put forward their best effort and accept the outcome. Such is the indomitable spirit of a true champion.

We've all seen real champions accept accolades with humility and absorb the blows of defeat with resilience. You too can use your victories to bolster your confidence and defeats as motivators. You can scrutinize each to discover what went right and what didn't. Then set a plan to sustain the strengths and improve the deficiencies. This is a way to move forward and improve while building resilience.

January 9

Amor Fati

Trust and respect everyone until they prove otherwise.

Be considerate and respectful of every new person you meet, and remember that you are also new to them. You do not want to be judged because of your race, gender, appearance, orientation, or station in life. You want to be accepted, trusted, and respected. So do they. Presume the best in people, and let them prove you right or wrong. Everyone, including you, will have ample opportunities to prove your worthiness or unworthiness.

January 10

Mortality

An abundance of people are willing to tell you how to live. Few show you how to live, and fewer still how to die.

In your life, you might encounter someone who transcends the norm and shows you rather than tells you the way. If you are exceedingly lucky, you might have the privilege of learning how to live and die by observing someone whose actions speak louder than words. Talk is easy and often easily forgotten. When you are in the presence of someone who is an example to emulate, you absorb and learn so much more. Finding those exceptional few who show you how to live honorably and how to die with dignity is truly special.

January 11

Emotion

Accord and harmony are transitory states whose duration and quality are determined by our focus.

We are predisposed for conflict, survival, and betterment. Our ability to refocus our energies toward harmony and accord reflects an inner strength and composure. This requires more focus and self-control than yielding to anger or fear.

Trust and believe in yourself. Find peace within yourself. Then, you can find harmony all around.

January 12

Awareness

Despotic, delusional, self-serving, and retaliatory are not the best words to hear describing a leader.

Throughout our lives, we encounter those who aspire to be our leaders, teachers, and life guides. We should not be blinded by their awe or hold them too high in esteem. Be aware of the words used to describe the leaders who seek your attention. If they are too glorified or too vilifying, pay attention, be prepared to be disappointed, and protect yourself. Such individuals are people focused on their own egos and aspirations.

January 13

Social Thought
Belligerence is not a virtue.

Anger, in and of itself, is a strong and often destructive emotion. When it is expressed in an aggressive and threatening manner, it becomes a force that disrupts the delicate balance of social interaction and moves into the territory of what is considered unacceptable. The act of vilifying and demeaning others, particularly those who are weaker or more vulnerable, is not an indication of strength, boldness, or bravery. On the contrary, it is a reflection of cowardice, a manifestation of the inability to engage with others in a respectful and considerate manner.

Recognize belligerence for what it truly is: a tool that is often used to manipulate others and to incite those who, for whatever reason, refuse or are unable to think critically for themselves. It's a tactic used to stir up emotions, to divert attention from logical and rational discussion, and to galvanize people into acting or thinking in a certain way. This kind of manipulation can be very effective, but it is also highly damaging and counterproductive to genuine dialogue and understanding.

Be vigilant in recognizing those who choose belligerence and bulling as their preferred means of management, communication, and manipulation. Choose your own path around them, and avoid being sucked into their delusionary nightmare.

January 14

Action

Conquer by force, and you strengthen a lifetime of burning hate.
Conquer with compassion, and you strengthen alliances forever.

History has many examples of successful and failed conquests. Successful ones forged alliances, ruled with compassion and acceptance, and brought the best of both societies together to create a better future. Failed conquests used brutality and force to dominate, punish, and control. In so doing, they fostered generational hate and revenge, burning in the hearts of the conquered.

The choice is yours. In your life and business, you can bring people along with you and grow together. Or you can plant the seeds of insurrection. The latter ultimately helps no one.

January 15

Problem Solving

Regardless of your expertise and experience, always approach everything with the eyes of a seeker and a beginner.

Be eager to learn, unencumbered by your knowledge, accomplishments, and habits. In every moment, there is something new around you to discover. Do not let the old, tired eyes of a sage blind you from new discoveries, opportunities, and adventures. View the world with the open eyes and excitement of youth, and watch your view and your wisdom expand.

January 16

Resilience

Your opinion of you matters most.

The concept is actually quite simple, yet profound: if you do not hold any belief in yourself, in your abilities, your potential, your worth, it will be nearly impossible for anyone else to do so. Your opinion of yourself, your self-perception, is far more significant and impactful than the opinions of others. It is the compass that guides your actions and shapes your life.

Do not fall into the trap of self-deception or self-defeat; instead, approach life with an optimistic honesty about who you are and what you can achieve. It's important to note that others may attempt to use their perception or opinion of you to manipulate and influence your actions or decisions. Do not let them hold this power over you.

Know who you are at your core, understand your worth and potential, and hold firm in your belief in yourself. Always, in all ways, believe in yourself.

January 17

Amor Fati

The only thing permanent in life is impermanence.

As you navigate the unpredictable journey of life, you strive to stabilize yourself, only for the vessel beneath you to begin to sway and tilt. You plant your feet firmly on the ever-shifting ground, trying to convince yourself of your stability amidst the uncertainty. You are but driftwood on the ever-changing currents of life, being rolled and turned, tossed and twirled in the relentless waves of change. The currents of existence are constantly changing, presenting new challenges and experiences.

Rather than resisting these uncertainties and changes and attempting to control the uncontrollable, embrace the unpredictability. You are an adventurer on the vast sea of life. Surrender to the ebbs and flows that define the human experience. Do not attempt to fight against the tide. Instead, find joy in the journey, relish the thrill of the unexpected, and simply enjoy the ride.

January 18

Mortality

Every day is not only one day closer to death but also another day of change and redefinition.

Who we were yesteryear or yesterday is not who we are today or who we'll be tomorrow. This applies to everyone, no matter their personality or life journey. Maybe you are a little stronger or weaker, more insightful or more closed-minded, more flexible or more rigid now than "before." You were what you were then; you are what you are now; and you will be different down the line.

Accept yourself today. Do not yearn for the you of days past or for who you dream of being in days to come. Focus on being your best *you* now, just as you are. If you want to change or redefine yourself, take some time and space to consider that possibility, but don't dwell on it. Be you and appreciate who you are today. Tomorrow, today will be history. Tomorrow and every tomorrow that follows will bring change.

January 19

Emotion

Hatred is a great evil, and ignorance is a great danger. Together, they form a toxin that spreads from person to person and is often fed to the masses to motivate them.

There are many ways to motivate an individual or to whip a crowd into a frenzy. By combining the evil energy of hate to ignorant and gullible minds, the uncontrolled vile power of the crowd is ignited. Be aware of those justifying their hate and lust of revenge as a protection for you. Be aware of your areas of uncertainty and ignorance, and educate yourself. Do not succumb to their poison. Instead, give aid to those weaker than yourself, as they are being seduced.

January 20

Awareness

Spare yourself from the self-inflicted suffering of focusing on things you know are upsetting and out of your control.

We all have enough suffering and disappointment brought into our lives by others. There is no reason to compound the frustration and pain by engaging in situations that are out of your control. This is especially true of situations involving other people, because no one other than yourself is within your control. Spare yourself this self-inflicted debilitating anguish by recognizing when something is throwing you off-kilter and stepping back from the situation, or even better, avoiding such disruptive situations altogether.

January 21

Social Thought

You give a little part of yourself to everyone you meet and everything you do. You choose what to offer; they choose what to take.

We are each a thread in the world's tapestry. We have a choice on the impression and impact we have on the people we encounter and the events we participate in. Amongst our many choices are to be gracious, compassionate, positive, disagreeable, disruptive, or alienating. That is what we, as individuals, can control. How we are perceived is the responsibility of those affected. However, their perception is just as important as our projection. Rather than stumbling blindly between perception and projection, focus on what you do and how you do it. Your actions will be more tangible, more salient, and less subject to interpretation.

January 22

Action
Be a model for emulation; take bold actions.

Even your smallest actions, when executed with boldness, are vital not only for your own progress but also for the impression you make on others. Bold actions serve as a powerful model that others may seek to emulate and repeat. Each action, no matter how small, builds upon another, creating a continuous cycle of growth and development. Over time, these bold actions become an integral part of your identity, shaping how others perceive you and making you a person others aspire to replicate.

On the contrary, timid actions can often be perceived negatively, serving as a model for manipulation and scorn, because they can project indecisiveness. Therefore, be bold in all your actions. Embrace your dreams and aspirations without fear or hesitation, for it is the bold who make history and leave a lasting impact on the world. Have Courage, Be Bold, and Never Fear the Dream.

January 23

Problem Solving

Critical thought does not seek to prove hypotheses; it seeks to disprove them.

Believing in something can make it feel easier to prove. Our subconscious minds naturally seek out information that confirms our beliefs while ignoring or dismissing anything that contradicts them. This confirmation bias often leads to a distorted and narrow perspective

Critical thinking focuses on proving things wrong. The practice of critical thinking takes a different approach. Rather than seeking to confirm our hypotheses, it focuses on disproving them. This is based upon the understanding that our beliefs and assumptions can often cloud our judgment, preventing us from seeing the truth. By actively seeking information that contradicts our beliefs and challenges our assumptions, we can break free from these biases and get closer to the truth.

Critical thinking is about exploring different perspectives and questioning everything. It's about not accepting things at face value but digging deeper and striving to understand the underlying mechanisms and principles. By proving what something is not, you gradually peel away layers of misinformation and misunderstanding, getting closer and closer to the truth.

You don't have to believe anything without employing your critical thought. Be willing to question everything before you declare your belief. And then, be ready to question your findings.

January 24

Resilience

How you perform each moment is how you will act every day on every task.

The effort that you consistently invest, moment to moment, creates a momentum that propels you forward and constructs a sturdy foundation for future endeavors. How you practice, whether it's a sport, a skill, or an occupation, directly translates into how you perform when it truly counts.

Concentrate on the task at hand rather than dwelling on past mistakes or worrying about future obstacles. Allocate time for thoughtful reflection and strategic planning. Then, dedicate yourself to performing to the best of your ability.

January 25

Amor Fati

Everyone is obediently doing their duty, as best they understand it. Even if their understanding is "wrong" in your opinion, they are still simply doing their duty. Just as you are doing yours, which in their opinion is wrong.

Challenge ideas, not people. Fate, in its unpredictable manner, sometimes places you in adversarial positions. These positions could be in a variety of arenas, such as business disputes, political debates, religious disagreements, or, in the most severe cases, military conflicts.

In these situations, you may find yourself honing and hardening your mind, body, and spirit. This is achieved by convincing yourself that your opponent is wrong and their viewpoint is flawed. In the best-case scenario, you may see them as simply misguided; in the worst-case scenario, you might view them as outright evil. But it's worth posing the questions: Are they truly so? Do they not believe the same of you? Yet, you know in your heart that you are not misguided or evil. Therefore, it's crucial to approach these adversarial situations with an understanding that it's the ideas that are in conflict, not the people themselves.

January 26

Mortality

Death is a transition, not an end. It is not to be feared, as it merely defines the limits of this life.

Many people are anxious about death. This apprehension stems from the belief that death is the final portal, a gateway leading us away from the existence we know once we've fulfilled the journey of this life. Death, in its finality, is the one common denominator that unifies all of our lives. Regardless of our perceived importance in society—the titles we hold, the wealth we've accumulated, or perhaps the lack of any of these—we all share one ultimate, inevitable destination. In the end, we all get to experience the same fate: We get to die. It is then, in our final moment, that we get our opportunity for transition, a chance to embark on a journey into the unknown that follows the cessation of our mortal lives. Accepting death as part of life gives you the chance to cast aside your fear of death. Then, rather than prematurely mourning the loss, you open yourself to enjoying the wonders of life.

January 27

Emotion

Our greatest wounds are not physical. They are mental and emotional, and most of those are self-inflicted.

The reluctance or inability to control our minds and emotions can lead to profound and deeply painful wounds. Our physical bodies are resilient, capable of withstanding traumatic injuries and debilitating diseases. However, the self-inflicted injuries resulting from an uncontrolled mind and unregulated emotions can be far more debilitating. These internal wounds, often invisible to the eye, can cause a level of suffering that far surpasses physical pain. Unlike physical wounds that heal over time with or without treatment, these emotional and mental scars can linger, affecting our overall well-being and quality of life. Wounds inflicted by an uncontrolled mind and untamed emotions can be a death blow, irreparably damaging our mental health and leading to a downward spiral from which recovery can be incredibly challenging.

You and only you can control your emotions and reactions. To guard against self-inflicted emotional wounds and distress, strive to understand, manage, and control your thoughts and especially your emotions.

January 28

Awareness
The attention you give something should be proportional to its worth.
Do not let the frivolous distract you from the essentials.

Time is one of our most valuable assets, and how we choose to spend it can greatly affect our lives. The same is true of our focus and effort. It is of utmost importance to be cognizant of the allocation of time, focus, and effort that you dedicate to all your actions, thoughts, and emotions.

Consider the ultimate value or end worth of your every action, thought, and emotion and ensure that you are giving each their proportional share of your precious time and energy. Be constantly aware of the trivial and frivolous things that may be drawing you away from what is genuinely important in your life. It is easy to get caught up in these distractions, but with conscious effort, you can steer your attention back to what truly matters. When you are mindful of how you spend your time and energy, you can lead a more balanced and fulfilling life.

January 29

Social Thought

Democracy's strength and weakness lies in our ability to engage in free speech. Now, if only we would listen.

The right to be heard might arguably be more significant than the freedom of speech itself. Freedom of speech represents our ability to express our thoughts, beliefs, and ideas without fear of censorship or retaliation. The right to be heard encompasses not only the expression of those ideas but also the reception of them. Our inherent desire to be heard is intrinsically paired with an obligation to listen to others. The concept of free speech, which allows for the expression of differing and challenging ideas, becomes meaningless in the absence of people who are willing and able to receive them, to hear or read them. It is through this dialogue, the exchange of ideas and the willingness to listen, that we as a society can grow and evolve.

It is better not to hear than not be heard. We all want to be heard—to be listened to and understood. As you prepare your counter to someone's statements, maybe you should be listening just in case they are agreeing with you.

January 30

Action
Some of the bravest people are those who simply say no

The strength to politely say no is probably one of the greatest acts of courage any person can perform. It is easy to say yes, to endorse and perform tasks you know are wrong, to be part of the group. Resisting the pressure of the crowd and peers to reject the common and blaze your own path is hard. Find your inner compass, dig deep, and bravely say no to concepts and actions that go against your ideals and better judgment. Be caught bravely saying no.

January 31

Problem Solving

Life can be hard and arduous while simultaneously being simple and joyous.

Life can be hectic and confusing. We find ourselves caught in the middle of a whirlwind of activities and decisions, which we perceive as all being of utmost importance. Time constraints bear down on us, and the pressure can be overwhelming. What we're confronting is the simultaneity of life, which we experience every waking moment. Life's challenges are thrown at us, and we're forced to juggle them as best as we can.

If you approach this with the right mindset, you can turn it into an opportunity rather than a hindrance. By focusing on one problem at a time, you can fully immerse yourself in the task at hand. This allows you to experience the thrill of rising to the challenge, of pitting your wits and abilities against the problem.

When you do find the solution, the joy you'll experience in that moment is incomparable. It is a testament to your capability and resilience, a validation of your efforts. These are the moments that make the tumultuous journey of life worth it. Solve troubles one at a time and savor the moment.

February

February 1

Resilience

What is inside you, good and bad, that you need to express? Your thoughts need to be expressed to clear your mind.

Your thoughts are like a wellspring that needs constant attention. Expressing positivity is like drawing water from a well, allowing fresh energy to replenish you just as fresh water replenishes the well. Venting negativity helps to release inner darkness and lighten your emotional load, just as removing debris from a well refreshes the water. If left untouched, the water in the well can stagnate and become foul over time. Similarly, unexpressed thoughts and emotions, whether positive or negative, can cause them to build up and stagnate, resulting in distress and dysfunction.

When you express positivity, you attract positivity, facilitating a natural replenishment that keeps you fresh and useful. Likewise, when you express negativity, it expels negativity from your psyche. Just as carrying something heavy in your arms can weigh you down physically, so can carrying a load of darkness burden you emotionally. By venting out negativity, you effectively lighten this emotional load.

Expression brings immediate emotional relief. It is also a vital part of maintaining your emotional health, just as keeping the water in a well fresh and clean is vital to its utility.

February 2

Amor Fati

Observe and accept life for what it is, not what you want it to be.

Life and the situations you find yourself in will encompass the breadth of the spectrum. You will find beauty and ugliness. You will experience pleasure and pain. You will have health and sickness. You will be happy and devastatingly sad. You will be flexible and adaptive. These are integral parts of the world and of you. Absorb all of them for the value and worth they bring. Yet, treat each equally, as they are simply part of life. You may be disillusioned as you face reality, but it is better than continually being deceived.

February 3

Mortality

Many people want to and will steal your time—your most valuable, irreplaceable asset.

Time, indeed, is your most precious commodity. It is bound by its limited nature, making it your most valued asset. Unlike material possessions, time is irreplaceable and fleeting, vanishing as quickly as it arrives. With an uncanny ease, time can be stolen from you, consumed by people who don't value it as much as you do or who squander time on trivial matters that don't serve your purpose.

The past is unchangeable and irretrievable, gone forever, although some try to rewrite it. You cannot travel back in time nor can you alter it. All that's left are the present and a probable future—how we spend our todays and our tomorrows. There is no guarantee how much time we each have left; there is merely the possibility of more time, making it even more precious.

Guard what time you have now and remaining. Protect it fiercely from those who seek to steal and waste it. Maximize its use in ways that serve your purpose and align with your goals. Do not let time slip away from you, underutilized or unutilized, for its loss is among the greatest losses in life. Remember, time lost is never found again. Strive to waste as little as you can, and fiercely defend whatever time you have left.

February 4

Emotion

Uncontrolled emotions, like evil people, can consume your freedom and render you defenseless.

It is a given that you, as a conscious and well-meaning individual, would never willingly let malevolent individuals, those with ill intentions and self-serving motives, take command of your life and your actions. These are the people who would insidiously infiltrate your personal sphere with the sole aim of manipulating you for their personal gain and not for your well-being. The notion of such an intrusion is something that you would actively resist and vehemently reject. Yet, many of us tend to allow our own emotions to rule us, to dictate our actions and decisions. That is when our emotions can become as controlling as self-serving individuals bent on harming us, influencing our behavior in ways that might not always be in our best interest.

Therefore, resisting and rejecting overpowering emotions with as much determination and vigor as you would use to ward off malevolent external influences is important. Learning to modulate your emotions is a crucial aspect of personal development and self-growth. The ability to do so is a hallmark of emotional intelligence. Be aware of the hold and effect that your emotions have on you and those around you. Control your emotions, and you will have more control over yourself and your life.

February 5

Awareness

The pain of repeating a tragedy or atrocity is far greater than the pain of the first offense. Now, you know better.

There will be tragedies in your life, some because of what you do, some because of what is done to you. The pain and sorrow can be overwhelming. Never believe or be fooled into believing you will be better if you forget. Remember the past; do not forget. Accept and acknowledge yesterday's actions and words.

But do not put yourself in a position or repeat the actions that resulted in the past offense, whether you were the victim or the offender. When a tragedy or atrocity is repeated, the wrenching pain will now be mental and spiritual as well as physical. You knew better, and yet you repeated your behavior. Learn from your experiences, or be destined to repeat them.

February 6

Social Thought

Can you accept who you are now and follow the dream of who you should and want to be?

You are who you are, whether you acknowledge it or not. For you to become what you dream of, you first need to accept your current you. Without self-acceptance you will be doing battle with yourself and all the other obstacles in front of you in your pursuit of your dream. An interesting aspect of self-respect is that it makes it easier for you to respect others. Self-respect helps you to disassociate yourself from emotions and attributes that are detrimental to you. It also helps you to develop the ability to intensely focus on your dreams without losing perspective of the world around you

February 7

Action

As a leader, while you should press to be firm, constant, and patient, you should also encourage curiosity, individualism, and initiative.

Strong, stable leadership requires you to be steady, insightful, and accepting while avoiding judgments that are skewed or corrupt. Lead for the greater good, not your self-interest, even if you believe your self-interest is the better good. Pierce your egotistical veil, and really lead. Encourage every individual to be curious and to have initiative. Great ideas can come from anyone at any time.

February 8

Problem Solving
Necessity has a significant impact on creativity.

The degree of necessity or desire for something significantly influences the problem-solving process, pushing it toward creativity and innovation. The greater the need, the greater the creativity must be. When common solutions do not produce the desired outcomes, it is a clear signal that it's time to reconsider our approach and think differently. Rather than viewing these situations as daunting, we should embrace them as opportunities for growth and improvement. There should be absolutely no constraints imposed on our dreams or our capacity to innovate. The power to dream is only as effective as our will to bring those dreams to life.

Let your dreams be limitless. Use your creativity to make those dreams reality. The journey from conception to actualization is a testament to your resilience and adaptability. Dream it, and make it happen.

February 9

Resilience

Short term goals allow us to experience the temporality of life. Long term goals give focus to temporality and drive us forward.

Goals, what one aims to achieve, are essential in everyone's life. Big goals are broken down into smaller, short-term ones. Realizing smaller goals gives you the sense of accomplishment and energy needed to move toward the next bigger task. They build your confidence, and you build your experience. Enjoy both the confidence you feel and the experience you gain in the moments you are in them, as they, too, are fleeting.

Goals need to encompass the three core aspects of our being: body, mind, and soul. *Unicentric* and *bicentric foci*, having a single focus or even just two points of focus, is not healthy or complete. Enjoy the opportunities and the thrill associated with setting and accomplishing goals. Always have goals, and strive to achieve them. You will improve physically, expand your knowledge, and push toward your own enlightenment. These are accomplishments no one can take from you. They are yours. You earned them; enjoy them and grow with them.

February 10

Amor Fati

What if, today, you started looking at everything as if you had never seen it before? What if, today, you looked at things like you will never see them again? You might then see it all differently, as if for the first or last time.

Accept where you are and the conditions life has given you. Look at things with curiosity and intrigue. Discover the uniqueness of everything you witness, and absorb it into your being. Like the waves crashing against the shore, each is different and yet the same. Each is simultaneously beautiful and dangerous. Each is seen once and never again, yet recurs repeatedly.

Would you see things differently if you knew you were simultaneously seeing them for the first and last time? Would you enjoy and relish each view differently? Do you see the grandeur or devastation? Could you see and appreciate both at the same time? What do your observations say about you?

You should be as observant as possible. The scenes you see will never happen again as you see them today. You should question not only what you see, but also how you it makes you feel because your perspective might be unduly influenced by your experience.

February 11

Mortality

You cannot lose either the past or the future. Neither is yours to hold; only today is yours to behold and experience. You have only the present.

Some people dwell in the past and on things lost or left behind. Others yearn for the future and dream of things yet to come their way. Yet, focusing on the past or the future both squander the only time any of us really have—today, the present, this moment. Leave the past behind you. The future is created today, not tomorrow. Today is your only opportunity to live and to build upon the past to create the future. Yesterday is history, and tomorrow is forever. Live in the moment; it may be your last.

February 12

Emotion

Desire clouds the judgment of most people and dictates their actions, rather than judgment affecting their desire and influencing their actions.

The concept of judgment, the ability to reflect on the past while simultaneously envisioning the future, is an example of *Janusian thinking*. Janusian thinking is the ability to hold and consider two opposing concepts in your mind simultaneously. This form of thinking allows you to make informed decisions that will ultimately influence your desires and actions.

When making a decision, be cautious of any emotions surging within you. They have the potential to cloud your judgment and distort your sense of reality. Desire, in particular, can be incredibly deceiving. It often acts as a blindfold, masking the truth of a situation. It's easy to get swept away in the currents of your desires, and resisting that temptation is crucial in situational awareness.

Do not let your passions overwhelm your sense of reason. Do not let bitterness and hatred dictate your actions. Instead, let your mind be the captain of your ship, guiding you through the turbulent waters of life. Keep your emotions in check and your judgment clear. Lead with your mind, and you will find that you can make rational, well-thought-out decisions.

February 13

Awareness

Whenever I encounter someone who feels they've never met someone their equal or superior, I pity the hellish, mundane, delusional existence they must be suffering.

Be aware: one's arrogance shows one's ignorance. The world is filled with amazing people doing extraordinary things every single day. The moment we think we're the best, along comes someone, somewhere who surpasses us. Consider, too, that one's person's norm is another's person's triumph, and one person's triumph is another person's norm.

You can always find people who are lesser than, equal to, and better than you, and you can learn something from every one of them. If you find yourself caught in the trap of arrogance, break free of your ego, stop measuring yourself against others, and open your eyes to the achievements and worth of every individual—including *you*.

February 14

Social Thought

There are no higher callings. Each of us has our own path. Each person's path is special and unique to them and essential in the fabric of society.

We hear many who claim to have a "higher calling." Consider their claim and those who propagate it with extreme prejudice. No one's "calling is higher (or lower) than anyone else's. A calling does not have to be spiritual, public service, or anything else. Everyone has a calling, and each calling is essential to that individual and critical to our society.

Take pride in your calling, and do it the absolute best you can. As long as you are on your path, stay the course. Be wary of those who try to make you feel inferior by lauding their higher calling.

February 15

Action

Moderate your pattern of expressing your opinion, and give full attention when listening to the opinions of others.

Some people spend an inordinate amount of time talking rather than listening. Continuously telling stories of your past or espousing your opinions is annoying and self-absorbed. Rather, listen to and connect with others. Do not make a habit of reliving your past; focus on living life now. Listen and learn from others with interest and patience, and share your opinions with calm passion and careful measure.

February 16

Problem Solving

The more complex the problem, the greater the need for diversity in finding a solution.

When faced with an extremely complicated problem, many people become reflective rather than collaborative. They think about how *they* can solve the problem and how *they* can orchestrate the situation. The best solutions, especially to complex problems, come from diverse ideas, not from on-the-same-page group thinking. Great leaders seek collaborators who have the intelligence and fortitude to be contrarian. Blending ideas is far superior to single-minded group think.

Welcome challenges to the norm. Think outside the box. Consider all ideas. Question, listen, discuss, and be ready to breech boundaries. The broader the solution base, the stronger the ultimate answer will be.

February 17

Resilience

We are the result of our past. Our aggressors are a reflection of their past.

Our past often shapes our future, and our experiences influence our actions. This is true for those who oppose us as well. Every day, we make quick decisions based on our experiences, knowledge, and passions, just like everyone else. Studying and understanding the past is important, as residual emotions from prior experiences can influence and predetermine our decisions today.

Try to understand the paths others have taken. Do not judge them or their path; rather, compassionately support them. Take a moment to ensure your decisions are not overly influenced by passion, as uncontrolled passion can create untenable situations. Avoid judgment and hatred. Instead, strive for understanding and compassion when facing your challengers, including your inner ones. Once the struggle is over, regardless of the outcome, support both the victor and the defeated. Focus on building alliances instead of animosity and hate.

February 18

Amor Fati

Every step along your path sets you apart from everyone else.

We are all a reflection of our experiences, past and present, and we are all uniquely different. Your path in life is yours and yours alone. While you may walk along a path with others for some time and distance, eventually your paths will diverge, creating a unique path for each individual. Along your way, you will also follow in other's footsteps and create steps for others to follow. Sometimes, you may walk alone, forging a path where none existed.

Don't underestimate the importance or the impermanence of each step of your journey. Accept where you are, who you are, and how you got there. Rejoice in your experiences, which are creating an incredibly special and unique individual ... you. There will only ever be one of you. Celebrate your individuality. Never sell yourself short. ... never!

February 19

Mortality

Death is life's greatest mystery and among life's greatest fears. We need not fear the unknown; we can embrace it with wondrous expectation.

Tell me what you know of death. The void of facts explains our apprehension of death. In this vast, intricate tapestry of life, we are presented with many experiences and events, death being the final one. Each new experience is shrouded in a layer of uncertainty, a fog that lifts only once we undergo an experience for the first time. Death, however, remains the last great unknown, a journey we undertake only once and without any guides or maps to lead us.

The inherent mystery of our death gives rise to a wave of anxiety that often feels insurmountable. It leaves us grappling with existential questions: Are we afraid of what we'll lose or face when we die. Or is our fear rooted more in the thought of how our death will impact those we leave behind, left to navigate the world without us? The former suggests a certain self-centeredness, while the latter hints at ego and our desire to feel indispensable.

Our legacy, the imprints of our actions and spirit, will remain long after we've departed. The echoes of our existence will resonate in the hearts and minds of those we've touched. Instead of fearing the unknown, we should lean into it. Embrace the wonder and unpredictability of forging a path you've never tread before. The unknown and unexpected are, after all, what make life so beautifully complex and endlessly fascinating.

February 20

Emotion

The resilience of water—placid when calm and calamitous when raging—should be our model. We can calm ourselves when chaos abounds, and we can create extreme change when we choose to move.

Water is so dynamic, just like our emotions. It can be placid, calm and soothing, yet flowing swiftly. It can also be a torrent, crashing on rocks and timbers. The water does not seem to care what state it is in. It simply responds to its environment, whether tranquil or turbulent, with the same ease, going with the flow. We learn from and emulate water. When our emotions are controlled, they carry us through life's challenges. When they are uncontrolled, they can carry us into mayhem, they can be our doom.

Endeavor to follow the way of water, to just be yourself, holding steady through the peaks and valleys of life. Respond to your environment as it is, not how you want it.

February 21

Awareness

You will inevitably transform during your life. When you are aware of these changes, you can prepare to optimize, counter, or adjust to them with purposeful effort.

Aside from the physical and intellectual transformation as you age, you will also change emotionally and spiritually over time, influenced by the environment around you. Be cognizant of the changes taking place. Some will be easy to recognize. Others will be gradual and insidious. Some will be a response to your physical and/or social environment.

Regardless of why and how you've changed, be aware and be prepared to take corrective action. You are responsible for who you are and for your response to your environment. It takes little effort to ease into a dire situation. It takes fortitude and confidence to pull yourself out. Regardless of how far down the path you are, if you find it is wrong, turn around.

February 22

Social Thought

The only person who has a right to judge you is you, and your right to judge stops at yourself.

Nobody is perfect. From time to time, we all need to take a good, hard look at ourselves and judge our actions against our values, abilities, and expectations. But no one else is qualified to judge you. You are the only one who has walked your path. No one but you knows how you got to where you are now or where you are heading. No one but you knows your whole story, even though some may think they do.

Likewise, you certainly do not know their story, who they are, where they've been, or where they're going. Judging others should make you feel extremely uncomfortable, not empowered. It is all right to listen to the judgers and their judgments of you, but take their assessment in the context of their knowledge of you. You will find most just don't matter. Follow your own conscience. Be fair and kind to yourself when judging yourself, and avoid the tendency to judge others for all the same reasons.

February 23

Action

Procrastination and indecision are corrosive practices. The day will pass, whether you engage or not. If you wait for everything to be perfect, you will never start.

We wait and wait. Waiting for the perfect moment to step in and take part. We hesitate and over-analyze, as indecision turns to procrastination. We invent self-justified reasons to delay. Rather, we should patiently assess and then engage.

Nothing will ever be perfect, so don't wait for it to be. Take a deep breath, know why you are going to get involved, and dive in. Begin at any level, regardless of how minor; just take part at some level. Any involvement is better than none.

February 24

Problem Solving

Tasks are part of life, but they should never become your life.

Our lives can be considered a series of interconnected, parallel, contiguous, and continuous tasks. Some we enjoy, bring meaning and reward. Others, we are simply compelled to perform, merely assignments in our lives. Such duty-calls tasks should never define our lives. They should be a means to an end, not an end to themselves. Life is short and precious. Pause for a moment, making sure the things you feel you must do are crucial and not just a duty. Don't *find* time for pursuits that enhance your life; *make* time for them. Make them a priority, and make time to exercise your body, mind, and soul every day.

February 25

Resilience
Life is a mirage and seldom what you perceive.

You are responsible and accountable for your actions. Diverse perceptions create a cloud of plausible denial, but this doesn't give you license to avoid your accountability. Even if others do not hold you to those standards, you must. Be the one who pierces the haze and clearly sees reality. Be the one who is true to yourself and others.

February 26

Amor Fati

Your preferred choice of personal characteristics should include stability, calm, and even serenity and excluding impatience, aggression, and chaos.

Even at the height of the storm, your composure and choices dictate your demeanor and behavior. Every violent storm passes. The crashing waves calm, and natural stability returns. So remain calm in every storm of life. Accept and embrace the turbulence. Find a way to calm yourself as calamity surrounds you and grips others, and lean into the chaos while calming others.

February 27

Mortality

You will not cheat death by hiding from your mortality or by living in the glory of your past. You will, however, miss the fullness of the present and squander your future.

Your past is your past, not your future. One aspect of your future that you can fully embrace is your death. Everyone and everything has an expiration date. Like me, you are no different than any other person or animal existing today. You cannot change that fact, no matter how much you try to hide from, ignore, or deny it. Your past glories cannot save you from the inescapable end of your life. Truth is, as we're reliving our past, we miss the wonders of today and forfeit our future.

However long or short your future might be, do not waste it on reliving and exaggerating your past. Let your past experiences allow you to find new pleasures in the present as your future unfolds in front of you.

February 28

Emotion

Humor is your last defense in the face of horror.

In your lifetime, you may very well see horror and experience tragedy. Like many people, you will face these atrocities with every fiber of strength in your body and soul, proudly and honorably ... until you feel you have nothing left. But you do; you have your mind and control of your emotions. You can also turn to humor to adjust your perspective and attitude. Smile and laugh at the situation you cannot control, but at least control yourself. Your humor will be unexpected and may give you an unexpected advantage. You may still succumb, but you will do it on your own terms.

February 29

Awareness

We are not as good as we think we are.

Our egos may very well be our biggest enemy. It is great to believe in yourself; self-confidence can foster growth and achievement. But some take it to the extreme, believing they are better than they are and superior to others.

Be aware of your strengths as well as your weaknesses, and keep your ego in check. Resist being self-absorbed, and vigorously scrutinize your own words and actions. *Not* doing so will blind you to your weaknesses, and your self-confidence will become a liability rather than an asset. Never flaunt your achievements or take them for granted. Always challenge yourself to be better, and be mindful, not boastful, of what you say and do. You will find it more gratifying and challenging to be superior at some things and recognize deficiencies in others than to be wallowing in mediocrity by being average at all things. Above all, take advantage of every opportunity to test and challenge yourself and to grow as a person rather than to inflate your ego.

March

March 1

Social Thought

Stupidity and incompetence wrapped in a religious blanket have caused more harm than pure evil.

Those who use any religion as a shield to spew hate and promote anger are amongst the vilest among us. These individuals embody the worst form of cowardice, hiding behind a false pretense of piety while they spread discord and division, feeding their message to the gullible for further propagation. It is our collective responsibility as members of our community and society to be vigilant, to be strong enough to pull back the deceptive veil they have woven. Truth is the greatest disinfectant against this treachery.

You have an obligation to call out this treachery and those who perpetrate it. You don't have to accept the travesty of cowards hiding behind piety. Be bold enough to shine the bright light of truth upon them whenever you can.

March 2

Action

It is wise to keep most of your words and thoughts quiet while in negotiation. Let those pontificating keep talking; they will reveal their intentions and ignorance no matter how hard they try not to.

Your silence can make the unconfident and arrogant expose their innermost secrets. Silence is uncomfortable for most people of this ilk. They cannot tolerate protracted, pregnant pauses in conversation or negotiations. In the face of a silent response to their bluster, they cannot help but continue to espouse their position and reveal their hidden intentions. Their well-guarded secrets and their private thoughts slip through the cracks of their carefully constructed defenses.

Remain calm and quiet; afford them the opportunity to lower their guard, to expose their vulnerabilities. Your silence does not mute your voice; it exposes and amplifies theirs. Remaining silent is not a passive act of withholding your words; it is an active strategy of shifting the dynamics of power in your favor.

March 3

Problem Solving

The brightest light comes from the inclusion of all light. Darkness comes by excluding light. Likewise, allowing and including all ideas and knowledge to come into the light enables us to discover the best ones. Leaving any ideas and knowledge in the dark prevents us from being the best.

Knowledge is not the exclusive domain of a select few. Neither are ideas and imagination. Seek out, solicit, and incorporate as many thoughts, ideas, and concepts as possible in your pursuit of knowledge and solutions. Just as history should be written not only by the victors but also by the vanquished, every piece of information and insight should be brought to bear whenever possible. Create the brightest light, just ask for an opinion.

March 4

Resilience

Do not be quick to believe and support. Press back hard against any tendency of gullibility.

Reserve your opinion and energy until you have enough information to make an informed decision. Enthusiastic promoters, along with their supportive followers, would like nothing more than to secure your commitment and belief. They prefer the mentality of the crowd and dislike the wisdom of the thoughtful. If their message and cause serve the greater good, their facts will stand up to scrutiny. Only then do they warrant your support. You are staking your reputation, so ensure it is for the right cause.

March 5

Amor Fati

Your uniqueness is what makes you special, and you should embrace it. Never succumb to the idea that your beliefs are superior or inferior to others; revel in the diversity of uniqueness among us.

You are unique. There has never been anyone exactly like you and there never will be. Your experiences, knowledge, insights, and collective understanding are as singular as you are. However, the things that make you unique are not superior to what makes anyone else unique. Each person, in their own way, is equally special and valuable. Acknowledge and celebrate these differences. Be intrigued by the individuality of others while accepting where life has taken you and where it will lead. Embracing the diversity of uniqueness paves the way for a broader perspective and understanding of yourself, others, the world, and life.

March 6

Mortality

We all age. Those who continue to challenge themselves physically, mentally, and emotionally will continue to thrive. Those who do not will atrophy in all aspects.

Amongst all of our fears, taking a risk is one of the biggest. Death is something you get to do; taking risks is something you choose to do. Take a chance, and push your limits. Challenge your body, mind, and soul as often as possible.

As we age, our challenges are different than in our youth. We all naturally regress as we pass our prime. This does not give us a license to quit. Quitting means giving up, and giving up prompts diminishment of all our abilities, and we begin to atrophy. As small or as big as the challenge might be, take the chance and try. You did it yesterday, so you can do it today, and so you might tomorrow.

March 7

Emotion

Failure and setbacks should be embraced as real opportunities to advance and grow.

We often grow more from failure than success. Attempting new things and facing setbacks or even failure gives us the chance to evaluate and make more significant improvements. We learn about the challenge, but more importantly, we learn about ourselves. Real strength and spiritual power originate from within, but only if we introspect. Acquiring these qualities requires dedication and focus. Once obtained, controlling them is an even greater responsibility and an opportunity for further challenges.

If you are open to it, you gain real strength and insight in defeat. Absorb the pain at the moment, and then in retrospect, critically assess what went right and, more importantly, wrong. You don't need to wallow in self-pity, as the difference between success and failure is often just the thinnest of margins. Pull yourself up, dust yourself off, and press into your next step of growth. You can do this.

March 8

Awareness

Pragmatism versus Perfection: You will never be perfect, and striving to be perfect will crush, disillusion, and disappoint you.

Consistent progress toward even the most ambitious goal will empower you. While you may aspire for perfection, it is an unattainable standard. No one, nothing, is perfect. It is essential to acknowledge that we all have limitations that prevent us from achieving absolute perfection. Embrace practical improvement, and accept the progress you have made. You have earned it.

March 9

Social Thought

We all have weaknesses, gaps in the perpetual armor worn every day, with the most pronounced being our self-interest.

Strengthen your resilience by managing your self-interest. Aim to think and act on a broader societal level. Beware of manipulators who appeal to your self-interest ahead of your empathy and gratitude. Recognize those who may exploit this potential vulnerability for their own benefit. They understand you are more likely to support their cause if they can convince you that it serves your best interest, even if it does not. This tactic is often favored over appealing to your empathy, gratitude, or initiating confrontation. Stay alert and be ready to accept that what serves your self-interest may not always align with the greater good.

March 10

Action

Pausing before reacting will yield perspective and clarity beyond rash action.

Passion and anger can cloud our judgment. Rash behavior seldom yields positive outcomes. Take a moment. Perhaps that's all you need to prevent an unfortunate decision. Actions require thought because they are irreversible and can alter the course of your future. You need perspective and clarity, which cannot be achieved when reacting in the heat of the moment.

March 11

Problem Solving

Only tasks worth doing well are worth doing.

If you don't think a task or project is worth doing well or to the best of your concerted ability, consider why you are spending your valuable time on it. What does "well" really imply? It means giving your best effort at that moment, on that day. You are aware of your potential, and you know when you optimize it and when you fall short.

Do things well, and take pride in the results. A sense of pride comes when you have given your all. Even if you fail, you can feel good about your attempt. While there will always be critics, do not be one of them.

March 12

Resilience

Make time each day to harden your body, expand your mind, and calm your soul.

Be available for yourself every day. No one else will prioritize for you, so you must. Make time and effort to take care of every aspect of your being—your body, mind, and soul. They all need nurturing, exercise, nourishment, and appreciation. Life's stress and commitments can often feel overwhelming and unending. However, these obligations will always exist and vie for your time and attention. The reality is, you cannot effectively manage your responsibilities if you are not physically, mentally, and emotionally equipped. Prioritize yourself first.

March 13

Amor Fati

For every problem, there is a solution—and usually more than one.

Life's problems are often intertwined with both known and unknown obstacles. No one can solve these complex problems, no matter how talented they are. However, by patiently dissecting and methodically resolving small portions, these problems can ultimately be solved. Accept and expect problems to come in all forms of interconnected knots, entanglement, and obstacles. With every solution, expect the unexpected. When obstacles arise, rise to meet their challenges.

March 14

Mortality

Everything created will either die or be destroyed. Enlightenment, however, is not created. It exists eternally and must be discovered.

Enlightenment, spirituality, and the search for quiet, calm inner peace and understanding are timeless. We understand everything created has an end. Enlightenment has never been a creation. It is a journey each of us is on, in our own way. It is a discovery ready to be found by anyone who seeks it, now and in future generations. Although enlightenment is universal, it is also very personal.

Be cautious not to criticize the path of awakening others are taking. Celebrate when someone you know or meet is on one. It is their path, and yours is yours. Focus on your path, or lose your way while worrying about it.

March 15

Emotion

Success and failure are supportive reflections of each other.

Celebrate your achievements with a sense of humility, fully aware that the opposite—failure—may come at any time. This humility in success is important, as it keeps us grounded and prepared for any potential setbacks. Conversely, do not be overly mournful or despondent in the face of failure. Embrace it, understand it, and learn from it. Failure, as harsh as it may seem, is an invaluable teacher. It provides us with opportunities to gain experience, to improve, and to build resilience. Remember: out of the ashes of failure, the phoenix of success may rise.

March 16

Awareness

Cognition, initiative, and humility are the cornerstones of leadership.

Strong, stable leadership is something we all yearn for in our managers and leaders, whether in business, politics, or religion. Real leaders allow and encourage others to stand out in the glory while shielding them when they falter. Real leaders avoid obtuse self-promotion and seek team recognition. Authentic leaders have a burning desire to improve their team and teammates. They are humble, yet self-assured, and they also believe in those around them. They help others rise rather than holding them down. Be wary of those who claim to be leaders but jealously covet fame while casting blame onto others.

March 17

Social Thought

Millions of people offering their thoughts and prayers will not change anything. Millions of people collectively raising their voices and acting together and independently will bring change.

We face numerous challenges today, as our ancestors did and as our children will. Often, we find ourselves feeling helpless in the face of these situations, listening to government and religious leaders lament about atrocities while offering their solemn yet hollow words to the victims and survivors. These individuals do not seek sympathy. They yearn for action to ensure no one else becomes a victim, and "thoughts and prayers" just ring hollow. While we are urged to keep victims in our hearts, this passive approach inevitably leads to more victims. Instead of merely talking, we should be acting. Thoughts and prayers will not bring about change; they merely create more victims. Change comes from raised voices and tangible action.

Rise and stand up for what is right. Lead with your voice, your vote, and your commitment to action, alongside the millions of others who aim to put an end to these senseless calamities.

March 18

Action

You are solely responsible for your actions and how you react to the circumstances that life presents you.

While you may not be in control of the diverse circumstances you encounter each day, the one thing you are indisputably accountable for is your reaction to them. Life, in its unpredictable nature, is neither inherently fair nor intentionally unfair; it merely exists in its own rhythm. In the course of your life, you may encounter obstacles of varying magnitudes. Some may be dauntingly large, others may be minor irritants, but all of them are inevitable elements of life. Do not shy away from them. Rather, acknowledge their existence and confront them head-on.

Your reaction to life's challenges is a choice entirely within your control. You bear the ultimate responsibility for your actions in the face of adversity. Ignoring these challenges or dismissing them out of hand is usually a recipe for exasperating the situation. Your response, especially to minor adversities, can be an illuminating reflection of your character. It is in these moments your true nature, your intrinsic qualities, become known. This is especially true when you believe nobody is watching you. However, it is crucial to remember that someone is always watching, even if that someone happens to be your conscience. So always act as if you're under observation, because, in truth, you are.

March 19

Problem Solving

There are three levels of truth: experience, reasoning, and knowing.

It is crucial to understand that absolute truth differs from personal truth, regardless of claims otherwise. Personal truths are shaped by individual perspectives, which are influenced by our life's lessons and amalgamated thoughts. Everyone has unique experiences and ways of rationalizing them. Some reason with logic, some with emotion, and others with a blend of the two. Even similar experiences can lead to different perspectives and reasoning, resulting in varied truths, even for the same experience.

There is a clear distinction between knowing and believing. Knowledge is founded on facts that can be proven and replicated. Belief, powerful but unproven, motivates us until proven incorrect. Practice tolerance toward others' truths; they may be nearer the absolute truth than you think and closer to the absolute truth than your truth.

March 20

Resilience

If something is worth the sacrifice, it is probably worth striving for.

We take so many things for granted today, including things that only a few years or generations ago were unthinkable and/or forbidden. Unfortunately, we may never fully recognize the efforts and sacrifices of generations before us, just as future generations may not appreciate ours. Value is directly proportional to effort and sacrifice. Only when we recognize the extent of the sacrifice to achieve something can we genuinely appreciate the value of the achievement. Not surprisingly, what we work for and earn has more value to us than something just given to us.

Take time to reflect on the benefits you have today. Acknowledge and appreciate the benefits you've generated and what you've given and given up to do so. Don't be concerned if others don't recognize your sacrifice; it was your choice and is your achievement, not theirs. Remember those who gave much—some, the ultimate sacrifice—so that you might benefit from their legacy and enjoy the moment.

March 21

Amor Fati

Personal faults are ours to control, subdue, and rectify. Those of others are theirs to manage.

Faults. We all have them, and they are all a matter of perspective. What you see in yourself as a flaw might be viewed by others as a strength. Vice versa, what you see in yourself as a strength might be viewed by others as a flaw. Likewise, others may view their own faults and strengths differently than you do. The faults of others are theirs alone to recognize and address, just as your faults are yours alone to recognize and address. Each person has their own journey of self-improvement to travel.

It is your responsibility to recognize, manage, and correct your self-deficiencies. In so doing, however, it is important to also recognize your own biases as well as the biases of others and society in general. Then, rather than beating yourself up for not meeting your own or others' expectations, forgive yourself, give yourself credit for your abilities and efforts, and reflect on how you might improve. Show that same grace to others who don't meet your or society's expectations, rather than blaming them for not measuring up.

Accept rather than judge. Allow yourself and others to follow your/their unique journey of self-improvement, unimpeded by your notions of fault.

March 22

Mortality

It is through your living, not your preaching, that your truth is revealed.

To those among us who exhort their personal beliefs and reject the personal beliefs of others: You cannot save our souls with your proselytizing words and judgment. When your actions do not align with your bombastic words, we deafen ourselves to your barking. It is audacious for anyone to believe they understand another person's journey better than that person does. It is insulting for anyone to claim their religious, spiritual, or moral superiority over another. The intolerance of differences and the rejection of diversity are a travesty in an ever divergent world that yearns for tolerance and acceptance. We live in a society with too much bigoted sectarian superiority and too little appreciation of alternate paths and positions.

There are many ways, many paths, to the top of the mountain. Let us find ways to lift people up and show ourselves not only through our words but also through our actions. If we are not, others may well wonder: *Are you proselytizing for our salvation or yours?* Let us find commonality in our beliefs and build upon those. Let us respect each other and rejoice in our common quest for self-realization and peace of mind and soul.

March 23

Emotion

Compassion is only useful when accompanied by actions that help make cruelty and suffering go away.

Compassion and caring are inherent emotions that a vast majority of species, particularly humans, exhibit. As social creatures, many of us often find ourselves deeply consumed by our innate sense of concern and demonstration of compassion toward one another. This care for others should not be confined to our thoughts, feelings, and words; it should be reflected in our actions as well.

Compassion should aim to relieve suffering and prevent cruelty. It is not enough to simply express sorrow and empathy, to simply offer "hopes and prayers." While well-intentioned, these platitudes often serve more to comfort the person uttering them than the person needing tangible help. At best, sincere expressions of compassion serve as a temporary balm. At worst, many are nothing more than sound bites spoken for effect and are hallow.

Real compassion requires action—a genuine willingness and effort to give support and alleviate another's distress. It involves stepping up to remove the source of their pain, whether that be physical or emotional. To truly embody compassion, strive to take action that brings about positive change, rather than merely talking about it.

March 24

Awareness

Two characteristics can be transformative in your life: the ability to say no and the ability to be spontaneous. At times, these transformative forces are mutually exclusive; other times they are mutually beneficial.

The willingness (mindset) and ability (follow-through) to say no and to be spontaneous can fundamentally change your life —provided you maintain your commitment to exercise them wisely and consistently. Without this continued commitment, you risk reverting to your starting point. Two such practices are: having the resolve to say no to, and having the spontaneity to say yes.

The ability to say no may be the most powerful tool for self-preservation. Many people and organizations demand too much of your valuable time. Protect it by simply telling them no. Do not let your time, money, and reputation be commandeered without careful consideration.

Embrace spontaneity. Be quick to assess risks, but also be ready to jump into an unexpected adventure with enthusiasm. Being spontaneous grants you the freedom to appreciate life's uncertainties. Your life does not have to be meticulously planned and structured. Occasionally, let yourself drift along with the flow of life instead of swimming against it. Try something new, relax and enjoy the ride.

March 25

Social Thought

When we realize we are all a part of humankind, we will evolve and transcend tribalism.

At the risk of stating the obvious, each person and every community is an integral part of humankind. But why is this fact so quickly forgotten as we self-divide ourselves into rival, angry tribes, each trying to exert dominance over the other at any cost, regardless of pain and suffering. Why are we so willing to judge and cast disparaging comments against others without fear of consequence or of harming others? Until we embrace the concept of global humankind and act accordingly, we will be forever in the grasp of tribalism. This will drag us down and may eventually take us all out.

It is possible to overcome the scourge of tribalism and the wrongdoing of discrimination, but it requires collective action: each of us acting together as one. Be willing to recognize when you find yourself thinking and acting like everyone else around you. For just a moment or two, try to put yourself outside their influence, and then decide their authenticity and validity.

March 26

Action

Small adjustments at the start are easier than major adjustments as your journey continues and ends.

In any project or on your life's journey, making small corrections at the beginning is better and more manageable than being forced to make major changes further along. It is important to understand that although early tweaks may seem insignificant, they can profoundly impact your path's trajectory. Every correction should make your journey smoother and more aligned with your long-term objectives. Any subsequent adjustment will require more attention, as the reaction time is lessened. No matter how far into the journey you are, if you find you are on a catastrophic route, it is better to stop and maybe turn around than to proceed.

March 27

Problem Solving

Dialogue enables thoughtful exchange of opposing viewpoints, but it requires focus on beliefs rather than personalities and sometimes exit strategies if they turn.

Civil discourse, constructive dialogue, and healthy debate are cornerstones of a free society. They offer the opportunity to present thoughtful opposing viewpoints on any subject, intending to find common ground and resolution. The focus of a discussion should be on the topic at hand, not on the individuals involved.

When the dialog becomes personal, it usually degenerates into an argument. Any party can start this personal attack, which can be overt or covert. This tactic is often used by someone whose argument is weak and who is losing the debate.

An emotional response to a well-formulated point and counterpoint can show immature idea development. The arguer, left with nothing substantive to contribute, resorts to disparaging personalized comments.

It is crucial to study the topic, which informs and strengthens your beliefs. Bring this knowledge and conviction to the discussion, and contribute your informed beliefs in a mindful, courteous manner. If a debate devolves into personal attacks or an emotion-fueled argument, you have a few options: You can try to calmly redirect the dialog to higher ground. You can moderate or withhold your comments; silence has profound and perplexing power. Or you can end the conversation, and just walk away.

March 28

Resilience

Conviction is a strength. So too is flexibility. While the willow sways and dances in the wind, a sturdy oak may lose limbs or topple.

Flexibility is a remarkable strength. Being flexible enables adaptability—the ability to maneuver in the face of unpredictability, challenges, and/or harsh conditions. Together, flexibility and adaptability, can be an asset. However, it is vital to remember that flexibility and adaptation do not equate to capitulation. Just as being too rigid can hold you back, so being too pliable can throw you off course. Learn to be flexible and to adapt to circumstances, without compromising your stance and direction.

March 29

Amor Fati

We can only understand the world and our lives by looking backward, but we must live our lives in the moment and plan by looking forward.

Living in the moment is beneficial ... to an extent; being too absorbed in the moment can be hazardous and myopic. Staying focused on the present while remaining aware of the world unfolding around us is an important and desirable learned skill. We should face what lies before us, use our past as a guide, and plan for what events might be forthcoming (a very Janusian perspective).

Many great leaders, in many disciplines have developed and honed this ability, which is often referred to as the "third eye." These leaders can execute their planned strategies while simultaneously assessing the scene playing out before them, foreseeing the scenarios yet to come, and then adjusting their tactics as needed. They avoid being so engrossed in one perspective that they become blind to the others.

Live in the moment and savor it. It will never occur again. But do not dismiss what you've learned or envisioned. Be cognizant of past influences, but not imprisoned by them. Be able to recognize the larger scene unfolding before you, but do not be distracted by it. Live in the now, aware of, but not susceptible to, what is behind and before you, and be ready to shift.

March 30

Mortality

Death is simply part of life. Fearing death steals precious moments of life.

How do you bid farewell to someone who is gradually passing away, their life slowly ebbing like the setting sun? You can do so by taking every opportunity to express your love in words and actions. You let them know they are valued and cherished and their presence has made a difference. You strive to fill their waning days with life—with what comforts, pleases, and is meaningful to them and yourself. You create precious moments to cherish—with them now, and in your memories after they've gone. The worth of these moments is measured not by their grandeur, but by the quality of love and care that fills them. In so doing, the fear and anxiety of death, both theirs and yours, is diminished by the richness of life in.

The same holds true when facing our own death. When we focus more on living and less on dying, fearing neither and finding peace in both, we are better able to accept our fate and make the most of the time we have left. We can live more fully and peacefully while we are alive. We can experience more priceless moments with those we will leave behind, creating memories that will reverberate in their hearts long after we're gone.

Such is the transient way of life. Do not let fear steal the most precious moments of life. Life is enriched by accepting the inevitability of death. It encourages us to embrace every opportunity to experience and savor life's riches while we can.

March 31

Emotion

Fear can enable or disable our ability to respond to a present danger. Anxiety can distort our ability to prepare for a possible but not always probable danger.

Fear is an emotional response to an immediate threat. Anxiety arises in anticipation of a threat that may never come. Fear is something you meet head-on, while anxiety quietly lingers, often just out of reach. Both serve a purpose—they alert and prepare you. But when misplaced or constant, they rob you of peace, focus, and the ability to engage fully with the present.

It's essential to discern whether you're experiencing fear or anxiety—and whether it's helping or harming you. If either begins to take over, pause. Center yourself. Examine the thoughts driving these emotions, and adjust your mindset accordingly. Fear, though intense, tends to be direct and short-lived. It's like a sprint—you face it and it passes. Anxiety, by contrast, is a marathon—it builds, loops through worst-case scenarios, and lingers.

Your internal alarm system exists for a reason. Learn to interpret it. Let fear and anxiety serve as guides, not captors. Face them with clarity, and reclaim your sense of control.

April

April 1

Awareness

The future is always uncertain. Assessing where you are on your journey is prudent, and it is all right to make course corrections. Staying the course can sometimes lead you astray.

Today, April Fool's Day, is a good time to consider the importance of paying attention to your surroundings. While April Fool's Day is about practical jokes played in jest, there are people who want to play you for the fool with malice.

Stay relentless on your journey, but be mindful of your progress along your path. Be aware of potential obstacles around and ahead of you. Keep your head up, scan the horizon, and occasionally look backward. The past has certainty not the future but it helps to know where you've been. This proactive approach lets you spot hazards well before they're at your feet. It is like rafting, where you constantly look downstream, adjusting your course to avoid upcoming obstacles. If you wait until you are upon them, it is too late.

April 2

Social Thought

Only the arrogant, egotistical, and foolish presume that all their thoughts, feelings, and actions are infallible.

Not everything anyone believes and does is "right," no matter how well-informed and well-meaning they are. Consider the possibility that at times you might be mistaken, even if only slightly. Respect and welcome, rather than debate or invalidate, the thoughts, emotions, and ideas of others. The wise can glean knowledge from every interaction. Maintain a sense of curiosity and enthusiasm for the perspectives of others. Embrace their ideas and comments without feeling threatened or challenged. Listen empathetically and ask questions to better understand their stance.

April 3

Action

Viewing life with a Janusian perspective, you can reflect on your past, be in the moment, and see where your actions are taking you tomorrow.

The future will cease to be a source of surprise if you make a conscious effort to simultaneously reflect on your past, ponder over your current direction, and evaluate your ongoing actions. Observation and introspection may seem passive to some, but in reality, these are two of the most proactive and potent actions one can undertake. These actions, despite their significance, are often overlooked by many and used by few.

Engaging in such reflective practices grants you a unique viewpoint and a sense of time that most people fail to appreciate or seize. Harness these tools to your benefit as often as possible. The understanding and foresight gained through such practices can provide a solid foundation for your future decisions. In fact, the trajectory of your future could very well hinge on these seemingly simple yet profoundly impactful actions.

April 4

Problem Solving

We always have time to delay tackling the hard things, and never have time to solve them. We squander time and effort on minutia, because we are afraid of the really grandiose things.

Procrastination, deferral, and denial are the tools of choice for those who do not want to face challenging issues. They will find distractions and excuses. They will pontificate the importance of the trivial that is consuming their time. They offer "thoughts and prayers" and empty gestures, instead of concrete solutions. Are they afraid of starting and doing the hard things or of failure?

Solving critical problems requires hard work, commitment, sacrifice, and risk. The solutions may not always be popular and may force us to confront realities we would rather deny. However, these are the issues, conflicts, and topics we must address, resolve, and solve with courage.

Are you one of the "they" that offer words of support but take no action? If you are not ready to face these challenges, step aside. You are blocking the path for those seeking to make a difference. Just get out of the way; you are blocking the path for those who want to deliver solutions.

April 5

Resilience

Body, mind, and soul constitute the three aspects of your being. It is unwise and unhealthy to surrender your mind or soul prematurely, as they can persist even if your body gives in.

Ironically, the hierarchy of the triad of your being—body, mind, soul—is presented in the order of their weakness. We know of examples throughout humankind where people have overcome unimaginable tragedies that debilitate their bodies while their minds and souls thrive. Their mental and spiritual strength sustains them through the morass, pain, suffering, and challenges.

To face and surmount life's battles, it is imperative to nurture each aspect of your being. A robust body can support a resilient mind and a serene soul for a considerable distance. However, as the body succumbs to injury or age, it becomes even more critical to fortify your mind and soul. They will continue to carry your whole being forward.

April 6

Amor Fati

We may or may not be able to control an event or its outcome. We can always control our reaction to it, and the most effective reaction is simply acceptance.

In the grand scheme of our everyday lives, we are faced with a multitude of factors, events, and circumstances that are simply beyond our control. While we may hold some degree of influence over these occurrences, we rarely hold the reins of control. Every event, from the trivial to the life-altering, comes with its own outcomes.

Even though we have no power to decide these outcomes, what we do have control over is our reaction to them. The ability to manage our reactions, to both the good and the bad outcomes, is paramount. This is where our true power lies.

Understand, too, that our joyous ending may mean a painful one for others. One person's gain is probably another's loss. This realization helps us to accept both good and bad outcomes as equal possibilities and imposters. They are not true reflections of our individual worth or abilities, but rather, simply the result of circumstances beyond our control.

Treat both victory and defeat with equal indifference. Doing so frees you from the emotional turmoil often associated with the ups and downs of life. It enables you to move forward without being unduly affected by factors beyond your control.

April 7

Mortality
A child's eyes are bright and full of wonder, while a senior's eyes are dim and tired.

Life's multitude of experiences and its relentless passage of time can often weigh heavily upon us. The ability to view the world around us with a sense of curiosity, wonder, and enthusiasm is the spark that keeps us truly alive. Seeing the world through weary, biased eyes serves only to cloud our vision, dampening our perception of the present and casting shadows over our anticipation of the future. The joys of life are not limited to any particular age or stage of life. They are perennial and can be experienced by anyone at any point in their journey.

Do not allow the hardships and exhaustion of life blur your appreciation of the wonderful gifts bestowed upon and available to you. Every moment holds the potential for a new revelation, every situation the chance for a fresh understanding, and every interaction the opportunity for a unique insight. All you need is the willingness to discover and embrace them. Strive to keep the spark of life in your eyes until the end. After all, it is this youthful spirit that keeps us vibrant, keeps us pushing boundaries, keeps us evolving, and keeps us young.

April 8

Emotion

The fears created by our imagination are greater than our reality.

Our imagination can be both a blessing and a curse. The anxiety we create in our minds can drive us to the brink of insanity. The delusions our mind can conjure can lead us to perform unimaginably illogical and emotional actions.

When distressed, ask yourself what is known and what is real. These are the things you need to deal with. All else is simply a product of your creation, terrorizing you from within. Take a moment to still your body and calm your mind. Give both your mind and body sufficient rest. Do not let physical fatigue fuel the tempest in your mind, nor emotional fatigue to wreak havoc on your mind. Give yourself a break—ideally before and always when you need one. Gather the clarity and strength to move on mindfully and confidently.

April 9

Awareness

Wealth is relative to need. Those who want little and have little are wealthy. Those who want much will seek to amass more and lose perspective along the way.

Wealth extends beyond mere financial accumulation. If your needs are met, you can find time for inner peace and social contribution. However, if your assets do not fulfill your desires, you may find yourself perpetually stuck on the hideous treadmill of desire. You run faster and longer, only to realize you are no closer to your desires, because the more you have, the more you want, regardless of your actual needs.

Jump off the treadmill of insatiably striving for external gratification; better yet, don't get on it. (Good for you if you've gotten off or never got on the endless cycle of want.) Strive for what you need, appreciate what you have, and discover all that life has to offer. The wealthiest individuals might, indeed, be those with the least financial resources.

April 10

Social Thought

We are social creatures living in dysfunctional societies, and the source of our greatest dysfunction are people.

What a paradox. As social beings, we thrive on interaction, yet the societies we build are far from utopian due to human influence. We live, breathe, and thrive within the complex structures of our societies, which, unfortunately, often just do not function. We are deeply embedded within these intricate social tapestries, which bring us both joy and pain. Yet, the dysfunction within societies often breeds considerable distress. Ironically, the root cause of the distress is people. Their diverse personalities and contrasting perspectives are sources of both our greatest joys and deepest sorrows.

You are an integral part of society. As such, you have a responsibility to try to function within the social norms, unless and or until those norms violate basic human rights. Then your challenge might be to become an agent for chaos.

April 11

Action

Obstacles and challenges serve as gateways and pathways to greatness. View these challenges as opportunities rather than barriers.

Life's paths are rarely straight or smooth. They are often filled with hurdles, bumps, twists, and turns, punctuated by brief moments of rest. These obstacles are an integral part of the journey. Avoiding one can lead to another, often larger, obstacle. Overcoming these challenges builds strength and confidence. Even in failure, there is growth, preparing you for future challenges. Success lies in facing these obstacles head-on. Failing to engage leads to certain failure. The path to personal greatness is tough. Embrace these tests, and grow stronger with each challenge.

April 12

Problem Solving

Only the morally, intellectually, or emotionally weak find scapegoats and make excuses. If you want the glory, you must also be prepared to take the blame. It is your responsibility to take ownership.

Do you often find yourself madly searching for a scapegoat? When it comes to taking ownership of unfortunate events or happenings, pay keen attention to what you do and what others do. Do you control your quest for achievements or possessions, or are you controlled by them? Be wary of becoming enslaved by the desire for achievements or possessions, which cause you to make excuses for your actions in pursuit of them or for your failure to obtain them.

Do not hide behind others by pushing them into the line of fire meant for you and your actions. Do not put your ambitions ahead of your integrity. Square your metaphorical shoulders, hold your head high and take responsibility. Accountability will always carry you farther than blame.

April 13

Resilience
If you do not take their money, they cannot tell you what to do.

There is an inherent dynamic of dependence and control between lenders and borrowers. Regardless of the circumstances, a financial debt creates a sense of dominance due to the obligation to repay. This relationship can strain even the strongest bond and jeopardize relationships, including family ties. This dynamic is not limited to individuals, but also extends to corporations and nations.

The lender often feels entitled to question the use of the money and the repayment schedule. They may also offer unsolicited advice or counsel, stemming from a sense of superiority. Meanwhile, the debtor may feel inferior, leading to irritation and resentment. The constant questioning and second-guessing of their decisions can further increase feelings of humiliation.

There is a way to break this destructive cycle. If you cannot lend without conditions, do not lend. If you cannot borrow without understanding there may be hidden strings, do not borrow. Avoid borrowing money whenever possible. Simplify your life, prioritize your goals, and live within your means. Do whatever you can to stay out or get out of debt.

April 14

Amor Fati

It is far better to be true to yourself; it gives you the luxurious freedom to worry less about what others think of you.

There is tangible power in being true to yourself, in having the self-knowledge and self-confidence to be the captain of your own life.

This superpower comes from becoming aware of and embracing who you are at this time—your strengths, weaknesses, beliefs, values, likes, dislikes, everything that makes you uniquely you ... today. Remember, the opinions of outsiders are just that—their perspectives and thoughts. They may try to influence you with their compliments or criticisms, but their comments are based on their experiences and biases, not on an objective knowledge of you.

Only through an honest assessment of yourself, recognizing where you excel and areas where there is room for improvement, can you truly understand your capabilities and potential. This awareness and acceptance of your true self serves as a foundation for personal growth and for navigating life's journey. Trust yourself and in the process of life having faith that tomorrow will unfold as it should.

April 15

Mortality

We walk the ever-narrowing path of life. Initially stabilized by love, we eventually find ourselves feeling unstable, alone, and without a safety net.

In the preliminary stages of our journey, our path is wide and exciting, seeming to offer limitless opportunities and experiences. We are stabilized by the powerful force of love and friendships. Their comforting presence guides and supports us, providing a sense of security and belonging and bolstering our strength to navigate the twists and turns life presents.

As we stroll further down the path, we find ourselves feeling increasingly unstable, our bodies and minds weakened over time and so many adventures. The once comforting presence of love may seem distant or has since passed away, and the secure feeling it once provided gradually fades. We may find ourselves sensing we are alone, navigating the treacherous terrain of life without a safety net, a stark contrast to the stability we once knew.

Be bold and have courage. Do not be too worried about yesterday's actions or too anxious about tomorrow. Enjoy the pleasures of today, because today is all we are assured.

April 16

Emotion

Anger consumes from the inside. Left to burn, anger overpowers the calm and clear thinking that prevents and relieves it.

Anger, one of the most potent and destructive emotions, requires careful management. Relentless anger burns hotter than any other emotion, scorching you from the inside and leaving nothing but the charred remains of your soul over time. It manifests in relationships and international conflicts alike, fueled by pain and suffering that gets passed from generation to generation due to our emotional immaturity and inability to let go of or extinguish it with reason and compassion. Anger outlasts pain, and revenge only accelerates the downward spiral, not just for the individual but also for humanity.

Recognize anger for what it is: a self-destructive and self-perpetuating harmful emotion. Guard yourself against it and its equally destructive counterpart, revenge.

April 17

Awareness

It is far better to go through life asking questions than expressing unsolicited opinions.

Throughout life's journey, it is advantageous to embrace an attitude of curiosity and exploration. This encourages us to perpetually ask questions, fostering an environment of learning and growth. It enhances our understanding of the world around us while promoting open-mindedness and respect for the perspectives of others.

Unsolicited opinions, more often than not, lead to friction, disagreement, and the impression of arrogance. It limits our personal growth, as it tends to close off avenues for learning and understanding unique perspectives.

While espousing opinions leads to alienation, asking questions leads to deeper, broader learning and understanding. It shows your interest in and respect for others' views. It allows you to broaden your horizons, gain new insights, and foster more meaningful relationships.

Consider being penurious with your opinions, and be prepared to ask a bountiful cornucopia of questions.

April 18

Social Thought

The world is richer when we all recognize and function as interlinked members of humanity.

We are all part of the same species, co-inhabitants on the same small planet. Regardless of our self-perceived worth, we are all born, bleed when injured, and ultimately die. Each of us is unique and integrally intertwined in the tapestry of humanity. Once we understand that the world does not revolve around us individually, both we and the world will benefit.

Allow people to be themselves, and perhaps they will allow you to be yourself. Show genuine interest in others, and they may do the same for you. We are all part of one family, and it is time we started behaving as such.

April 19

Action

If there is no internal fire, no amount of encouragement will light your passion.

Any idea you can imagine can be a goal. However, without the personal desire to materialize the goal, it will remain a dream. No one else can drive your passion as effectively as you. Without your desire, no one can ignite the flame required to push through the trials and setbacks necessary for success. Without passion your burning fire is easily extinguished. You must have the desire yourself.

Do not give up. Remember, creativity requires movement and energy, while stagnation leads to squalor and decay. Start fresh each year, each day, each morning, ready to apply your efforts to your passion, to create your future.

April 20

Problem Solving

The bigger the issue to be resolved, the broader the diversity of input needed to resolve it.

Problems often present themselves as complex interconnected knots, entanglements, and obstacles, seemingly insurmountable no matter how keen the observer or how sharp the mind. Such challenges cannot be solved in their entirety in one fell swoop, no matter how desirable that may be and possible that may appear. However, they can be progressively unraveled by patiently analyzing, meticulously dissecting, and systematically resolving smaller, more manageable parts one at a time.

It is important to acknowledge that no one person holds all the answers. We find the most effective solutions, more expediently, by seeking help, through pooling of knowledge from diverse minds. It is the synergistic effect of diversity that can often provide the most elegant, innovative, and effective solutions to seemingly impossible problems.

Seek out and incorporate as many potential solutions from as many diverse sources as possible. Encourage an open dialogue, encourage the sharing of ideas, and do not shy away from seemingly outlandish suggestions. Complex issues warrant a diverse and multifaceted range of solutions, each one contributing a little piece to the grand puzzle. Often, the whole is greater than the sum of its parts. Many diverse minds can slice through the most complex Gordian knot.

April 21

Resilience

Knowledge and wisdom are gained through experiences and observations.

Knowledge and wisdom, akin to progress, are gradually and painstakingly acquired. It can be challenging to persist when gains or rewards are minimal. Significant achievements are not the result of a single act, but rather the accumulation of consistent, mundane efforts.

Pursue opportunities and challenges that offer the best potential for learning and enriching experiences. Learning is the initial step in acquiring knowledge. Then apply these lessons amidst life's challenges and obstacles in your quest for knowledge and wisdom.

Put the books aside. Turn off your computer. Set your AI-driven device aside. Step beyond their contained pages and programmed solutions to experience life in all its beauty and ugliness. It is in this realm that you will gain experience, knowledge, and wisdom.

April 22

Amor Fati

Prepare for the various storms in life—both nature's and those caused by humanity and yourself.

In a tempest, secure yourself mentally and then physically. If you do, your mind will carry your load even as your body starts to yield. If you do not, you will be unprepared for the challenges ahead and you will falter.

Although you cannot change the circumstances you find yourself in, you have the capacity to logically assess, understand, and accept it, which gives you the capacity to navigate through it. Acceptance is not surrender, resignation, fatalism, or capitulation. It is a dynamic act of gauging and preparing, embracing the reality of the situation and acting within it to your advantage.

Prepare your body, mind, and soul for the onslaughts, obstacles, and challenges that arise. Transform these storms into opportunities, and you will find beauty and tranquility in them.

April 23

Mortality

Merely extending life without considering quality of life is demeaning, harmful, and evil.

Modern science and medicine have advanced beyond our moral understanding of the implications of extending life simply because it is possible. There is value in curing diseases, saving lives after severe trauma, restoring or improving health, and preventing illness. The value of preserving life merely for its own sake is, at best, a questionable and misguided goal. Keeping the body "alive" without considering the essential failure of the body and/or mind can border on cruel. Yet, our moral standards often prevent us from considering alternatives.

There comes a point when both the body and/or mind deteriorate beyond repair. A strong mind can thrive even in a failing body, and a strong body can thrive with a failing mind. Either way, suffering ensues and escalates. Both the body and mind degrade, leading to a loss of self-control over both, often without dignity. Extending life for the benefit of the individual can be a blessing or a cruel curse. Extending the life of another for selfish reasons should be morally repulsive. We should focus on living well while we can instead of trying to unnaturally extend life.

April 24

Emotion

Moral strength and spiritual power come from within. Obtaining them takes commitment; controlling them is an even greater responsibility.

Moral fortitude and spiritual tranquility cannot be purchased. While some might try to sell them, they are inherently personal and cannot be bought. They arise from deep within and are unique to each individual. Developing these qualities within yourself requires commitment and focus, effort and patience. Controlling them is even more challenging and a greater responsibility for which you are accountable. Tranquility is found from within and then expressed outwardly. Self-calm and composure can only be achieved with peace of mind. Control your mind to cultivate moral strength and spiritual power.

April 25

Awareness

The further you pursue your spiritual path, the more distant and independent you become from the influence of group followers and charlatan leaders.

Determine your own spiritual laws and avoid blindly following others, simply echoing their words or ridiculing others. Your beliefs are just as valid as theirs, and they are personal to you. Be aware that there have been and will likely be fraudulent imposters claiming to lead people to spiritual enlightenment. Their gods cannot protect or punish you; instead, protect yourself from the collective mindset and the greed of such charlatans. Your spiritual journey is yours alone. Disregard those who ridicule you or others on their paths, and keep a healthy skepticism. Maintain your own counsel in a crowd, and be comfortable in your silence. If someone genuinely seeks your insight, be open to sharing, as they may be truly interested.

April 26

Social Thought

No one knows everything, but everyone knows something worth learning.

Opportunity is constantly knocking and the wise are those who hear it. Often, the opportunity is simply to learn something from anyone and everyone. Even those whom society deems lowly can teach us something, but only if we're unbiased and open enough to listen and learn. Many of last century's theoretical truths are mocked today, just as ours may likely be ridiculed a century from now.

Be open to all ideas and beliefs, but be selective about what you internalize. Once an idea has taken root, it can be hard to dislodge. Do not hold your ideas and beliefs, nor those of others, as supreme or absolute. Examine and challenge every "truth," before dismissing or embracing them.

April 27

Action

We can learn from the sages of the past, but we expand our knowledge through what we discover and apply today.

We can and should advance on the shoulders of giants, not be held back under their oppressive boots. Rather than worshipping and adhering strictly to the ideas of our teachers and mentors, we can and should forge new ideas and surpass them. Those who cling to old ideas undermine not only themselves but also the intentions of their revered thought leaders.

Do not allow yourself to be imprisoned or stifled by the thoughts of people who are dead or whose knowledge is obsolete. Let them be your guides, not your masters. Use their lessons and your mind to blaze new bold ideas, forging new directions and discoveries for next generations.

April 28

Problem Solving

Understanding the question is the first step toward finding the answer.

When you encounter a new problem or task, take a moment to digest it. Resist the impulse to immediately jump to a presumed solution or response. It is all too common for people to provide inaccurate or ineffective solutions, simply because they have not fully comprehended the question or problem in the first place.

Seek to gain a comprehensive understanding of the issue at hand before trying to address it. Practice patience and thoughtfulness in your approach. Be meticulous in understanding the nuances of the problem. Only when you are confident that you fully understand the challenge you are facing, should you continue to formulate and offer a solution.

April 29

Resilience

With knowledge of how, we can repair. With understanding why, we can improve.

Knowledge is split into two categories: the answers to the question of how, and the answers to the question of why. *How,* refers to practical knowledge for maintaining functionality, which is vital for successful operations. *Why,* delves into the rationale behind design, separating innovators from users. It is key to unlocking potential and surpassing original capacity. It challenges the status quo, striving for improvement and breakthroughs. While how enables management, why fosters innovation. Knowing both ensures smooth operation and enables the creation of groundbreaking concepts.

Understand how something functions as well as its purpose. Study its structure, mechanics, and design parameters. Then think of adaptations which can enhance its functionality, flexibility, and extended utility.

April 30

Amor Fati

Disasters and catastrophes are not the vengeful acts of a god or evil acts of a fiend. They are simply part of nature.

Human history is replete with myths, folklore, and superstitions, often used to explain or assign blame for natural disasters and catastrophes. These events are more accurately viewed as the random chaos of nature, not the vengeful acts of any deity. Actions lead to reactions, resulting in the unpredictable outcomes of nature. Instead of blaming a deity or demon, we should accept that both positive and negative events occur naturally, that some are accidents, and some are our own doing.

You cannot prevent or change natural and unforeseen tragedies. You can only accept and embrace their reality. But, you can prepare for most of them. Ironically, those we do not prepare for are often the ones we attribute to anything and anyone but ourselves. Nothing is predetermined in the course of life. Everyone makes their own way in life and lives with the consequences.

May

May 1

Mortality

Knowing yourself is more important than understanding others. Only by piercing the veil of self-deception can we truly know ourselves.

Why do we invest so much energy in analyzing and judging others, yet devote so little to self-reflection? We often hide behind a self-created and self-serving veil of self-deception. Before attempting to understand others and their motives, we must first understand ourselves.

Remember, you are an amazingly unique individual. Find joy in your uniqueness and spend time introspecting. By knowing and accepting yourself, you will find peace of mind and be better equipped to accept others. Judge yourself fairly but honestly. Celebrate your strengths while setting plans to fortify your weaknesses. It is also far better to spend time critiquing yourself than judging others. Self-calm and composure can only be found with peace of mind. Tranquility within can then be projected out.

May 2

Emotion

Mental health is as vital to our well-being as physical health.

When we are physically ill, we're likely to rest, tend to our malady, and/or seek treatment. So why don't we do the same for mental illness? Why is there such a societal stigma associated with mental health issues? Mental and emotional instability and disorders can be as, if not more, debilitating than bodily ailments and traumas. They can also be infectious. You can suffer from another person's psychological or emotional misery, just as you can be uplifted by their positive mental and emotional states.

It is essential to prioritize your mental health as much as your physical health. Make sure to rest, stay calm, exercise, and nourish your body, mind, and soul. Don't hesitate to ask for help. Your life may depend on it.

May 3

Awareness

Life is a mixed bag of the good, the bad, and the neutral. And it's all a matter of perspective.

Sometimes things go wrong. Reflect on a particularly bad day, and ask yourself whether it was the entire day or a single event that triggered the negativity. Often, it's a single event—a bad conversation, traffic ticket, bad news, or other annoyance. Consider how you reacted to the event and whether your reaction impacted the rest of your day. A day filled with great events and interactions can turn sour because of your overreaction to a single, maybe unrelated, negative event.

Letting a single event or string of events control our day or our life is not beneficial. Accept that bad things happen. Acknowledge that good things happen, too. Feel your pain or distress, but find something positive in every situation. Pushing aside either negative or positive feelings can distort your perspective, which controls your mind and reactions. The dark and the light are both part of each day, of every life. Face and process both your negative and positive emotions, then let them go and grow through them.

May 4

Social Thought

A plethora of people are eager to tell others how to live. Scant few show us how to live, and fewer still who show us how to die.

Many self-proclaimed experts are eager to advise us on how to live our lives. They eloquently elaborate upon what we should or shouldn't do without ever knowing anything about us. However, only a few truly exemplify how to live through their own actions. Being a role model is far more challenging than merely pontificating and proselytizing. Even fewer role models have the chance to show us how to live life to its fullest and confront our mortality.

We should pay attention to the people whose lives are examples, rather than those who simply market their advice like a common product. Seek out and pay attention to those willing to show rather than tell. They are the very rare gems of life.

May 5

Action

Criticism is effortless and questionable, particularly when the critic offers no solution.

Countless naysayers lurk in the world, and being a critic comes with enticing ease, particularly when one is not burdened with the expectation of performance. Beware of vocal bystanders who offer opinions but no solutions. Be the one who offers proactive measures for solving the problem or achieving the goal.

Begin by thoroughly evaluating the issue at hand—the complexities, nuances, and different perspectives that surround it. Once you understand the problem, brainstorm, research, consult with others, and tap into your own knowledge and experiences to identify the solution. Plan and fine-tune the solution. Take tangible steps toward implementing your solution, no matter how small or seemingly insignificant they may be. Every action matters. Assess and adjust actions as needed, and follow through until the mission is accomplished.

May 6

Problem Solving

A wise person strives to constantly expand their knowledge, and learns from everyone and everything they encounter.

Learning is impossible for those who believe they know everything. Every task, experience, and interaction with another person has something to teach us—regardless of its seeming insignificance or unpleasantness.

Position yourself as a lifelong learner. Be someone eager to absorb and analyze the surroundings and situations you encounter. Someone eager to understand and consider the teachings and philosophies of anyone at any time, regardless of their status in life. Everyone's experiences are unique, and you can tap into them if you're truly open to learning. By learning from others' experiences, you can gain insights without having to go through the same situations. The more you know, the more you realize what you don't know. Strive to constantly expand your knowledge.

May 7

Resilience

Character is your most powerful defense in a world where there are those who would love to tempt, change, manipulate, and crush you.

You can prepare for the various storms of life—of nature, from humanity, even self-inflicted ones—in many ways. You can equip your body, mind, and soul to withstand these onslaughts. But have you fortified your character to weather the blows? A weak character corrodes all of your other attributes, making you vulnerable. A strong internal moral compass and resilience are vital when facing a powerful storm, especially when others falter and you begin to follow.

Knowing deep down who you are and what you stand for is an unconquerable force. Your character is and always will be your most powerful defense, even against those who want to control you or see you fail. When your body and mind start to yield and your soul quivers, it is the strength of your character that guides and sustains you.

May 8

Amor Fati
Think about what you think, not what others think.

We often find ourselves more concerned with what others think than with what we think. We worry about what they think of us and our thoughts. We try and figure out what they're thinking, especially with regard to something we care about—be it business, politics, religion, parenting, whatever. Sometimes, we are so consumed with thinking about someone else's ideas that we don't give sufficient attention to our own. Ironically, they are probably worrying about what you're thinking too.

When you spend more time thinking about what you think, your thoughts and deductions are crisper and more forceful. You are more confident and comfortable with your ideas, your decisions, your actions, and yourself. Consider all thoughts while concentrating on your own and formulating your own opinion.

May 9

Mortality

Awareness of death begets a deeper appreciation of life. Awareness of life begets a greater acceptance of death.

Each of us embodies many dualities: ignorance *and* understanding, timidity *and* courage, insecurity *and* confidence, self-indulgence *and* self-discipline. These juxtapositions are unique to and co-exist within each person. The two sides of a duality are both contrasting *and* connected, which helps to keep us challenged and balanced.

The extreme embodiment of duality is the juxtaposition of life and death. Each is an inverse image, a reverse reflection, of the other. How we perceive life and death will affect how we live our lives. We can look at life and death with a blasé or distorted perspective, in which case we're likely to be unsatisfied with life and uneasy with death. Or we can look at life as an adventure to experience and death as the end of a well-lived journey and possibly the start of the next.

Embrace and make the most of every day, every moment of your life. Create memories and establish your legacy, to serve others after you're gone. Live as purposefully and fully as you can while you're alive, mindful that death is part of and the inevitable end of life's journey.

May 10

Emotion

To some degree, we are all self-loving narcissists. We would all benefit by turning our self-love to empathy and caring more for others.

There is nothing wrong with taking pride in who you are and what you've achieved. However, when pride and the quest for attention become your sole motivations, it can lead to self-centeredness. Such a mindset can shift your focus from others to yourself, creating an unhealthy balance. Instead, use your energy and self-love to empathize and care for others. You might be surprised by the amount of love you receive by prioritizing others. Remember, you are not the center of the universe. Do not think you are. By keeping this in mind, your influence may grow beyond your expectations.

May 11

Awareness

While each day may seem endless, time is finite and can be either used or wasted.

Time is more than just a measure of our existence; it is a precious asset and a powerful ally. It allows for plans to be made, goals to be achieved, and dreams to be realized. Time is an invaluable but limited and finite resource. Each passing moment is a fragment of time that can never be reclaimed. As time unfolds, it offers a continuous flow of opportunities and experiences as well as diversions and disruptions. Time is a precious gift, and it is up to each of us to squander or maximize our time.

Don't let time get away from you. Be mindful of time's relentless passage and aware of distractions that waste time. Seize each moment, and make it count, investing your time in pursuits that enrich your life and the lives of others. Amidst a world of continual distractions, stay focused on what matters. Time is yours. Use it wisely.

May 12

Social Thought

We reveal our perceptions at the risk of being deceived by those with concealed intent. And withhold them to protect our intentions from them as well.

Perception is an individual's unique take on an idea, situation, experience, themselves, or another person. In so doing, we observe, evaluate, and sometimes judge through the lens of our training and experiences, often with little or no regard for other viewpoints. Perception is crucial to understanding many things, including the human desire for deception. Often, people do not want their true intentions known. They hide their motives, hoping others will not perceive their ulterior motives. Someone's interest in your perceptions can be a deception to hide their intent to mock or block your idea. Conversely, deception can prevent your intentions from being sidelined or exploited by others.

We live in a world in which self-advancement is common. Unfortunately, greed and power can be strong motivators to those who seek advancement, particularly those who are weak-minded and of poor character. By understanding their viewpoint, you may be able to mask your intentions, becoming invisible from their perspective.

Scrutinize everything from various angles, particularly from the inside out. Be aware of those who seek to gain from undercutting you. Disguise your intentions to make them invisible to those with the wrong perspective and visible to those with the right one.

May 13

Action

Acta non verba. Deeds, not words.

Impactful, successful people tend to act more and talk less. Rather than boasting about their achievements, they let their deeds speak for themselves. While many enjoy sharing their tales of conquest and success, if what they do doesn't embody what they say, it is just empty talk.

Perform your duties quietly, unassumingly, and confidently. Focus on planning, preparing, and executing your next task. Ensure your actions have a purpose and your words meaning. Going through the motions is like rubbing a stone to make a mirror. As with empty talk, it's a futile waste of energy without any substantial results. Instead, strive to do things well and take quiet pride in your accomplishments. Those who matter will recognize your efforts, while the rest will continue talking.

May 14

Problem Solving

The power of repetition is potent, whether used to strengthen or weaken.

Study and practice relentlessly. This advice is common in athletics, education, professions, the arts, and other pursuits. The frequent, ongoing repetition of beneficial and increasingly demanding actions can fortify your body and mind to tackle greater challenges. Consistently exercising and eating nutritiously, for example, builds an athlete's strength, stamina, and skill.

On the other hand, continual repetition of an unhealthy behavior is inherently destructive. A lie, for example, if said often and loudly enough, can transform into a perceived truth, especially in the minds of the uninformed. This false narrative can ruin the integrity of societies and families, tearing us down and apart. Some things aren't worth repeating over and over again, and some aren't worth repeating at all. Resist repeating what doesn't work or might cause harm. Use repetition to build yourself and others up.

May 15

Resilience

What we invest in love, hate, or life is what we receive in return.

The choice is yours. Your time and energy are at your disposal, and you determine their allocation. The quantity and quality of time and energy you invest in love, hate, or life itself will reflect in the results. Significant time and dedicated energy will yield substantial returns, while the opposite can result in neglect and dismissal. This principle holds true for love, hate, and life in general. Time, energy, and focus will produce results.

Consider whether you're improving to impress others or to satisfy your own pursuits. Why spend time on the fleeting reward of merely impressing others? Instead, invest your time and energy in yourself, in love, and in life—and you will reap tangible and enduring rewards.

May 16

Amor Fati

Circumstances change, and we change. Sometimes our perceptions, actions, and even our direction changes accordingly. Yet, each person's path remains their own.

Generally, you get to choose your life's path. Along the way, obstacles or situations arise that divert you from your current path. Sometimes these diversions are a detour leading you away from and then back to your chosen path. At times, they might lead to a new path, just as a river changes course to refresh itself. In a constantly evolving world, it is essential to adapt and adjust to new circumstances. However, adaptation should not be an excuse to take shortcuts or wander aimlessly.

Whether your path or circumstances lead you to another path, it is still yours. Seek to understand its fundamentals, remember them, and practice regularly. No matter your skill level, sticking to the basics will lead to success. As you navigate the challenges of your journey, give it your best effort, make peace with your mistakes, and take pride in your efforts and achievements. Aim for self-gratification and self-improvement rather than external recognition. After all, the only person you need to impress is yourself.

May 17

Mortality

The fear of entertaining new, challenging ideas comes at the cost of stifling and withering the mind and soul.

A stagnant mind is no better than a dead leg of an oxbow lake. A part of the channel, once the area where ideas and concepts swirled around and intermingled, is now choked off from the river and dying a slow, miserable death. When we become mentally timid—reluctant to learn new concepts or challenge ones we've held for years in fear of being opposed or ridiculed by others—we become our own stagnant pond. We stop being inquisitive and begin to decay. Our minds and souls slowly die from a lack of curiosity, investigation, analysis, opposition, and trial and error, which are the keystones of critical thinking, learning, and growth. Clinging to our comfortable old mindsets and beliefs, never questioning ours nor exploring others, will eventually be the root of our demise.

Your life's stream needs to keep flowing. It needs the influx of tributaries to bring new ideas into your mainstream. Accepting additions, even if murky and silty, to be blended into your consciousness and experiences. You flow faster and stronger with more resilience.

May 18

Emotion

In solitude we move between quiet contemplation and social engagement. In isolation we shield ourselves within our own private, self-absorbed world.

There is a difference between solitude and isolation. Both are choices. Some people take pride in their ability to thrive in solitude, using that quiet time for self-reflection and self-care. They come back to society with increased self-assuredness and inner peace. Isolation can have vastly different, often damaging effects. Those who intentionally or unwittingly isolate themselves may become self-reliant to an unhealthy degree. They may become so fixated on their mindsets and beliefs that they reject other possibilities and become delusional. This self-absorption can grow increasingly destructive.

Avoid prolonged isolation. If you find yourself stuck in insolation, strive to break free of its chains, even if that means seeking help to do so. Seek and make time for solitude and self-healing, and always return to society. Although society can seem chaotic, it is part of human life and exists to serve you. Your mind will re-engage and adapt, and you will grow.

May 19

Awareness

Whether cast in elation or spite, words cannot be unspoken or unheard, and actions cannot be undone or unfelt.

Individuals might tolerate egocentric people, provided they remain polite and cordial. However, if in their bravado and egotistical rants they insult, ridicule, demean others, their words burn in the hearts and minds of those attacked and their witnesses forever. If they are abusive, threatening, or hurtful in their words and/or behavior, their actions will also be fodder for their downfall.

During euphoric states of self-congratulation, remain mindful of what you say and do. Be aware that words and actions can wound and leave scars. They live forever, outlasting all of us.

May 20

Social Thought

In any religion, it is inexcusable for punishment to be the alternative to faith. Spirituality is greatest when it allows and encourages the utmost freedom to follow, question, and modify.

Faith and spirituality are individual choices and pursuits. A person's faith and spirituality are extremely personal and belong to them alone. They should never be subjected to ridicule, harassment, or any form of mental or physical punishment. Rather than judge or criticize we should accept and appreciate their unique journey. Any religion that advocates peace and harmony, yet chastises, mocks, or incites violence against those following a different path, reveals its hypocrisy. We must recognize and call out such for what it is and such hypocrites for who they are.

May 21

Action

Authority increases with each action that inspires trust and respect.

With greater authority comes the greater need to inspire trust and respect in those you lead. This is comparable to a flywheel; once started, it is difficult to stop unless there's a catastrophic failure. The more authority you possess, the more you need to be cognizant of your impact on others and to consistently earn their respect and solidify your authority.

Observe empathetically the impact your authority has on others. Be mindful of the potential pitfalls of increased authority. The more you possess, the more autocratic and rigid you may become and the less open you might be to new ideas or approaches. Age and experience can potentially lead you down a detrimental path of self-absorption and self-adoration, resulting in the loss of your authority. Be vigilant against these destructive pitfalls, for the sake of both those you lead and yourself, lest your flywheel spins out of control.

May 22

Problem Solving

Procrastination and indecision are corrosive practices. The day and the moment will pass whether you engage or not.

In problem solving, as in daily life, procrastination and indecision are two of the most harmful practices. Things will never be fully understood or perfectly planned. If you wait until they are to engage, the problem will be solved by someone else and the opportunity for you to contribute to the solution will pass you by. When this becomes a pattern, you will marginalize yourself in the eyes of your colleagues, leaders, and neighbors and earn a reputation of indecisiveness and weakness.

There is much to be said for the axiom, "Do something, even if it is wrong." Don't wait for everything to be perfect; just participate at some level. By taking action, you might determine more about the problem than by doing nothing. A small, calculated step can yield great results with acceptable risk. Step forward and take action every day.

May 23

Resilience

Prepare for the various storms of life—nature's storms, those of humanity, and self-inflicted.

Can you turn the foulness of defeat into fertilizer for success? Like manure, we can often use something we initially see as disgusting to help us grow stronger. Storms and turbulence are around us all the time, many of which we knowingly and unknowingly create ourselves. As distasteful, disappointing, or disastrous as the storms of life may be, they present wonderful opportunities if we are prepared.

Prepare your body, mind, and soul for the onslaughts of life. You will find inner calm, strength, possibility, and value in them. Find a way and means to use their strength to your advantage.

May 24

Amor Fati

The more you know, the more you realize how much more you do not know.

Imagine drawing a circle on a piece of paper. Inside the circle represents what you know, and the circle defines your limit of knowledge. The area outside the circle represents what you don't know, the unknown. You study hard and you experience as much of life as you can. You draw another circle and recognize it is bigger than the last one you drew. You know more and have experienced more. Looking at the two circles, clearly the boundary between your known and the unknown is now greater. You also realize that although you know more, what remains unknown to you still surpasses what you know. You realize that the more you know, the more you know you don't know.

Recognize the current breadth and accept the current limit of your knowledge and skills. Then strive to fully utilize and expand them through concentrated effort. There is no limit to how much you can learn, and the quest for knowledge is lifelong. Expand your knowledge circle as far and for as long as you can.

May 25

Mortality

Life should be measured not by its duration but by its achievements.

A short life filled with accomplishments, regardless of their magnitude, is more valuable than a lengthy but unfulfilling life. Focus on the present task and enjoy every moment. Playing by someone else's rules may limit your personal achievements. Understand who you are and your goals. Set an objective, devise a strategy, and tactically work toward your goals. Regardless of how far along you are on your life's path, continue to learn, plan, and act. Share your experiences and find happiness along the way, even if it is small or hidden in hardship.

May 26

Emotion

You don't need financial wealth to appreciate life. In fact, it often impedes appreciation. All you need is gratitude for life's bountiful beauty.

Life's beauty is freely available to anyone who seeks it, and there is an abundance of beauty in life to discover. The riches of life are accessible to anyone and everyone, always. Ironically, those who relentlessly pursue monetary wealth and glory, impetuously toiling to accumulate fame and fortune, usually miss out on the amazing things life offers. An unchecked desire for wealth often breeds misfortune and misery, not fulfillment and gratitude.

Desire is the yearning and quest for things the person wants but might not need and/or be willing to share. Real wealth is having and appreciating what you need and being able and willing to share it. Each day is unique and presents another chance to seek, appreciate, and share the abundance of good stuff life has to offer. Simplify your life and your needs, and control your wants. Then enjoy the splendor of the world around you in its amazing grandeur and subtle beauty. Enjoy and appreciate every moment.

May 27

Awareness

The reality of reality can be harsh and invigorating, simultaneously.

Be aware of and don't be fooled by masks people wear as they create their life's mirage. Instead, watch and study their actions and character. The facade created by people's dress and demeanor is often in defense of their own insecurities and weaknesses, but sometimes it is also or instead intended to seduce you into a vulnerable position. With observant and discerning eyes and ears, watch, listen and try to decipher what it actually means. Pay attention to tangible details, and do not be swayed by images. Their mirage is intended to hide their strengths and weakness.

More importantly, do not fall for your own facades. Being fooled by someone else is unfortunate; being fooled by your own false image is unforgivable. No matter how perfect the projection or reflection, it remains a reflection of what is real, but it is not real. Be aware of who you are and are not. Be you. Be real.

May 28

Social Thought

There are many paths and many means to enlightenment. Once there, you understand the path and means don't matter as long as we are all on a path.

Spirituality and enlightenment are unique to each person, a reflection of that individual's experiences, mindsets, and beliefs. The paths and means people take in the quest to attain and retain spiritual enlightenment are highly personal and sacred. No one has the inside scoop on anyone else's path to spiritual enlightenment nor the right to criticize, disregard, or prohibit it.

Determine your own spiritual path, principles, and practices. Hold on to them, and do not be swayed by interlopers. Avoid adherence to a flock of followers, mimicking what they hear and mocking others. The more you follow your own spiritual path, the further away you are from the masses and from the influence and control of charlatan leaders. When someone has chosen a different spiritual path than yours, don't critique or discount it; respect their perspective and rejoice in their journey. Stay quiet in a crowd unless someone seeks the benefit of your words. Stay true to your journey while you celebrate others on theirs.

May 29

Action

Embrace where and what you are with grace and humility while fiercely and proactively making changes for improvement.

Embrace the situation you find yourself in *(Amor Fati)* with a positive mindset, but don't confuse this acceptance with capitulation. Acceptance is an active decision that enables you to take action; surrender is allowing the actions of others to influence or determine your reaction.

Acceptance is acknowledging the present reality while actively preparing to make the future better. It is embracing where you are at the moment and using that as a launching pad to elevate yourself to where you want to be. By accepting your circumstances, you achieve a level of clarity and peace of mind that allows you to harness your greatest strength: your ability to focus sharply and intently.

It is important not to wish for or actively seek conflict or calamities. Life will inevitably present these challenges; when it does, meet them head-on with strength, honor, and humility. Accept these obstacles for what they are: realities that need to be confronted, not lamented. When accepting these challenges, prepare yourself to face them. This doesn't mean becoming combative or confrontational. Rather, it means equipping yourself with the necessary tools, knowledge, and mindset to effectively deal with these challenges.

May 30

Problem Solving

Trust is always earned, and trust is a matter of action, not perception.

Collective strength is an asset and a key factor in the success of any relationship, team, or organization. Trust in oneself and in one's partner or colleagues fosters cohesion, forming the glue that holds the unit together. With trust, each member's strengths, skills, knowledge, and even weaknesses come together to form a formidable force. Without trust, weaker members may feel vulnerable and stronger ones may feel superior, leading to internal conflict. While feigned trustworthiness can be used as a facade to gain favor, genuine trustworthiness can build strong bonds within a team. Trust is built on the honesty, sincerity, and integrity of each member of the unit.

Be as honest and sincere and act with as much integrity as you can, and people will trust you. Endeavor to associate with people who display their honesty, sincerity, and integrity. Avoid those who pose as trustworthy individuals but are not. We all walk with someone or some team or another through different legs of our life's journey. Find those you can trust. Be a person others can trust.

May 31

Resilience

Obsessing about what we need and want is confining. Living within our means and needs is freeing.

Listen to the voices of spoiled children. Hear with disgust and dismay as they whine for their "I wants" and boast about their "I haves." Ask yourself: Do I have everything I need or everything I want? The first addresses your common needs to live. The next addresses the pursuit of non-essential niceties—the things of desire, the items that can be broken, lost, and/or stolen.

Clearly, you need certain things to survive and to live a secure life. Recognize that acquiring and longing for anything beyond those things can become an obsession, and uncontrolled obsessions are often the root of misfortune. Strive to eliminate "I want" and "I have" from your mindset and vocabulary. Free yourself of unnecessary desire and bondage to things that can be destroyed or stolen.

When so many around us need so much, it is better to appreciate what you have and work for what you need. It is also wise to recognize that sometimes you need to let go of what you have in order to gain what you need. Living within your means and needs gives you a freedom and independence no one can take away from you.

June

June 1

Amor Fati

Anxiousness is allowing things out of your control to consume your attention and energy.

There is something evil about anxiety. It lurks in your mind and feeds off your self-perceived weaknesses. It can consume you and returns only more self-doubt. When you are fatigued, it emerges more vicious and becomes stronger and more viral, draining and paralyzing you. In this state of mind, things beyond your control consume your attention and energy, sucking you into a black hole of persistent worry and unease. This relentless cycle of anxious thoughts and fatigue erodes your positive energy and self-confidence, giving nothing back but more anxiety.

Pause and focus on the facts in front of you, not on worries about what was or might be. Parse what is real or possible and what is imaginary or exaggerated. Control what you can, and accept what is not within your control. Break the spiral of anxiety with rest, nutrition, exercise, and proactive preparation. Calm your mind with the knowledge of who you are, what you have done, and what you are capable of. Believe in yourself, and manage your anxiety by facing your fears, putting them in perspective, and focusing on now.

June 2

Mortality
Fear not death nor the fear of death, for if death is the end, it is also the end of fear.

One universal truth is certain for every living being on this planet: our inevitable mortality. No matter our status, wealth, accomplishments, or connections, we are all bound by the same fate: death. And many people fear death. For some, it is the fear of death itself—the end of existence, the cessation of consciousness—that frightens them most. For others, it is the fear of the unknown, the uncertainty of what lies beyond, if anything at all. The fear of fear is an inherent part of human nature, a primal instinct.

If we consider death to be an end, it must also signify the end of our mortal fears. If so, there should be no fear, anxiety, or uncertainty. One could argue there is genuinely nothing to fear from death. We must ask ourselves, is there truly anything to fear about death, or is the fear itself the only thing we have to fear?

June 3

Emotion

Niceness does not equal goodness. Only genuine niceness does good.

There are many personal character traits, but being "nice" is not one of them. Being nice is a decision—a choice each of us makes as a strategic action of social interaction and engagement. In this world, there are good people and bad ones, either of which can choose to be nice when it is to their benefit. Niceness is a mask we all wear occasionally with good intention, such as taking the higher ground in a challenging situation. It can also be used to mask ill intent, such as "making nice" to deceive or manipulate others. Deciding to be nice, indifferent, grumpy, mean, or any other of the demeanors we have at our disposal is up to each of us. Maybe we should try to be genuinely nice more often. Perhaps it will stick and become a trademark we can live up to.

June 4

Awareness

The brocade of our lives is woven by the interlacing threads of success and failure. True success requires knowing the sting of trial and failure and overcoming both.

Don't let the fear of failure prevent you from taking on new challenges. Failure forms the base of the performance pyramid. The wider the base, the higher the potential for success, as long as you keep trying. Quitting after failure only harms your self-esteem and perpetuates a sense of failure. Those who have never experienced failure have not truly pushed their limits, and thus, in essence, have never experienced success. Success is built upon a cycle of failure and triumph. Much like loading and unloading strengthens your muscles, this cycle develops mental and physical resilience and stamina.

Your life's fabric is woven from the intertwining of failure, success, and the mundane. Without failure, success feels empty and superficial. Yes, failure brings pain, suffering, and disappointment. However, these experiences enhance the thrill, validation, and reward of success, giving us the energy to persevere. This energy transforms the pain into the exhilaration of achievement. Embrace both success and failure, as they strengthen the fabric of your life.

June 5

Social Thought

Religion and spirituality are related but not synonymous. Religions are the creation of people and cultures. Spirituality is a personal and unique relationship with oneself, nature, and creation.

We are expected to gather like sheep at our preferred house of worship. There, we listen to a teacher describe how we should live and what we should believe according to the religious doctrine. We are told their religion is superior, the "right" one, and all others, even sects based on the same religious manuscript, are false and dangerous. The message: Believe, or leave and be condemned. Believe, or be damned. Yet, those same organizations have a history of hypocrisy. Many religious leaders succumb to the sins of flesh, money, and power, seeing themselves above all others, including their parishioners. Their piety is surpassed only by their hypocrisy, which is echoed by their flock.

Rather than chastising, preaching to, and trying to convert others to our religion or spiritual path, let's focus on transforming ourselves. Let's not be chained to the structure of religions. Instead, let us seek our own spirituality by whatever means we choose, whether in solitude or in community with others. Likewise, let's accept the religious or spiritual beliefs and practices of others, without judgment or interference.

June 6

Action

The only things between you and achieving your goals are commitment and effort; and you control them both.

In a fundamental sense, the only thing standing in the way of your goals is you. Of course, there will be obstacles and impediments imposed by outside factors. Those are to be expected when setting your goals. But it is the abundance of your patience and commitment that will determine how focused your efforts are in your quest. Patience and unwavering persistence will be your shield and hammer in breaking through limits and making way for possibilities. Failure becomes an option when either your commitment and/or effort begin to falter.

It may be convenient to blame others and try to avoid accountability; however, these are your goals, not theirs. You took time to define your objective, lay out a strategy, develop tactics and specific actions, and focus on putting them into action. Retain your vision and passion while calmly learning and preparing for the setbacks and hurdles you will inevitably face. Be impatiently patient and relentlessly persistent. You control your commitment and effort, no one else.

June 7

Problem Solving

If good food smells bad, it's likely to be deemed bad and passed over. The same applies to ideas and opinions. If they don't pass the "smell test," they're likely to be rejected even if they are fundamentally good.

Every day, countless brilliant ideas fail to be sold or implemented. Often, this isn't a reflection on the concept or opinion itself, but rather on how the idea is presented and to whom it's presented. Audiences are more likely to embrace a radical opinion if they perceive it holds value for them. Conversely, if an idea doesn't resonate with them or they find no value, the idea and opinion will be dismissed without ceremony.

A key part of ensuring the success of an idea is the ability to clearly articulate its purpose, process, and promised outcome. That requires you to identify and listen to your audience or consumers. Their perception is critical to its success, so their perspectives must be addressed. If they sense something amiss, that the idea "smells" wrong, you need to find out why. Once you've identified the issue(s), you need to address them and eliminate the metaphorical "stench." If this isn't possible or if the idea continues to be poorly received, it might be time to seek out a different audience or consumer base for your idea or to rethink your idea.

June 8

Resilience

Strong yet flexible bonds are forged with the warmth of commonality and the heat of honest, respectful disagreement.

We are social animals. We crave connection with others and flourish when we have friends and are part of organizations. Your friends, associations, and memberships are also important components of how you are perceived and received.

Be aware if an association, whether a person or group, which demands you surrender your independent ideas and ideals. Critically evaluate the situation, the association, and your participation. Individuals and groups that accept only "like minds" and are closed to different views care only about themselves.

Never surrender your individuality or your ability to voice an opinion or take a direction that differs from someone or a group you associate with. Be able to step away with grace. No association is more important than your independence and your reputation. Be the person you believe you need to be, even if it means being alone. Forge alliances with people and organizations that allow, respect, and seek to learn from the commonalities and differences of others.

June 9

Amor Fati

Truth is true only in a moment of time and in the eyes of the beholder.

An absolute truth exists, but it is valid only at a particular place and time, influenced by perspective. To understand this truth, you must be willing to accept and consider everyone else's viewpoints. Truth is a kaleidoscope of shifting images with varying degrees of bias and ambiguity. Reason and truth are present but often obscured by our biases and preconceived notions. This distortion is amplified by our common reluctance to appreciate others' perspectives. They are seeing the same thing but from a different viewpoint, which is not necessarily incorrect.

Consider a perfectly cut diamond. The way light reflects and refracts from it changes based on your viewpoint and the lighting conditions. The pattern of light you observe differs from what the person next to you sees. Both of you are captivated by the same dazzling gem but perceive it differently. The same applies to absolute truth. Be mesmerized by its kaleidoscopic sparkle, and strive to seek it out. Embrace both subtle and overt perspectives in your quest for reason and truth within nature's ever-changing existence.

June 10

Mortality

Life is a one-way journey with an unscripted, unpredictable destiny. Every decision, every choice, regardless of size, sets your course.

There is no predetermined destiny in life. None. No one is destined to do this or be that. While there are many influencing factors out of our control, it is how we react to them and the decisions and choices we make every moment of every day that sets and steers the course of our lives. We, by our own thoughts and actions, determine our destiny.

Setbacks and calamities happen. How we deal with them matters. How we strive to avoid them matters. Details matter. Every day, you make countless small decisions and choices. Each is a link in the chain of your life. Each is somehow interconnected and influences the next choice and the choices yet to come. Each choice matters. They determine your destiny. You create your own destiny by your choices, decisions, and actions.

June 11

Emotion

Guided by our inner purpose, we weather life's storms and discover the sea of serenity.

A sense of purpose is fundamental to our living a fulfilling life. Without purpose, that inner compass that steers us toward what is meaningful to us, we often find ourselves floundering, adrift in the vast sea of life. This state of aimlessness can lead to distress, discontent, and lethargy. When we discover what gives our life meaning and follow that path, it leads to serenity, contentment, and vigor. Knowing the path is right for us, we navigate through life with clearer intent and direction, more deftly adjusting course as required by unpredictable circumstances.

Find your why, if you haven't already, and endeavor to live up to that purpose every way you can. Your purpose will give you the presence and peace of mind to allow your intentions, convictions, and positive emotions to guide your decisions and actions. It will also calm and center you when the going gets rough. Stay true to your purpose, secure in the knowledge that living purposefully enables you to create and experience even more beauty in your life.

June 12

Awareness

Piety and hypocrisy are a toxic cocktail, intoxicating minds with their emotions and moods rather than facts and analyses.

Beware of charlatans posing as teachers and leaders, offering a mix of piety and hypocrisy but no answers or solutions. History is resplendent with them. They present themselves as our champions and saviors while living lives contradicting their own teachings. They hope we'll be too intoxicated by their toxic elixir to see through their grand charade.

Pay close attention to those in or wanting influential roles. Don't be swayed by emotions or the dramatic praise from those around you. Instead, focus on the facts and the thorny issues, equipping yourself to stand firm and independent. Hold these charlatans accountable, even in the face of potential harassment and threats. It's better to sober up than to continue drinking their vile intoxicant.

June 13

Social Thought

When we serve others with grace, the world is a better place and we are better for it.

Have you noticed that those who have much often flaunt their riches and rarely give without bravado? Have you also noticed that so many people have so little, some barely surviving?

We can and should do better. Here are three simple social practices we can all follow:

1. Selflessly help others. Give our time, money, whatever we can to those in need, with no expectation of reward or recognition.
2. Face personal hardships with courage, confidence, and grace. Rely upon ourselves and own resources to resolve our problems and relieve our suffering, leaving assistance resources for those who desperately need them.
3. Share our bounty with those who are less fortunate. There is plenty to go around if we do not selfishly hoard and covet more.

If the majority of us followed these basic life practices, none of us would face anything alone. We would all have the support and necessities we need. We would all be better prepared to move forward together rather than apart as the haves and have-nots.

June 14

Action

Nothing is gained from pointing fingers, shrugging shoulders, or walking away. Everything is possible when responsibility is accepted, action is taken, and accountability is demonstrated. Nothing is gained from making excuses or finding scapegoats.

In a world full of people who are quick to point fingers and slow to solve problems, be the exception. Become a part of the kinship of individuals who take responsibility and act decisively. There is a deep-seated respect and admiration for those who choose this path and a common disdain for those who do not. Be the person who actively seeks out solutions rather than dwelling on the problems or blaming others. Show the maturity to be accountable for your actions, whether they result in success or failure, understanding both are a part of personal growth and life's journey. Stand tall, act responsibly, seek solutions, and be accountable. This will set you apart and make you a beacon of reliability and maturity in a world lacking both.

June 15

Problem Solving

The best decisions and actions are derived from the union of personal wisdom and collective thought.

Your knowledge and experience are amazing resources upon which to base your decisions and actions upon. Trust in them and study, learning even more. Never forget there is another great resource around you all the time: the knowledge and experience of others. Solicit and listen to their advice. Tap into it while you weigh their self-interest. Be wary of suggestions leading you astray.

Decisions and actions resulting in destruction and resentment are typically not well thought through and often conjured in a silo, without research, inquisition, and input from others. They may be technically correct while practically false and misguided. Live in the world, observing and evaluating, growing your knowledge and experience for betterment. Solicit the counsel of others with the ability and intention to contribute. Remember, a cornucopia of unique, diverse ideas builds the strongest position.

June 16

Resilience

Our only true possessions are our mind and our soul. They are also our most valuable assets.

Why do we fiercely protect our things and bodies yet easily surrender our minds and spirits? Unchallenged minds and spirits can atrophy, leaving us stagnating in a pool of familiar but stale ideas and concepts. Chronic neglect of mind and soul inhibits our personal growth and can drown our curiosity, confidence, and ambition. Constant challenge, even if it's uncomfortable, is a preferable alternative.

Allow your mind and spirit to wander, explore, and forge connections. An unwavering focus on obsessions, dramas, or injustices can lead to a monotonous mental fixation. Break away from such fixations and open your eyes to the wonders around you. Seek a sanctuary, a place to rest and silence your mind and spirit to life's constant noise. Quiet focus on what is within rather than around you allows your mind and spirit to open, freeing your mind to explore and your spirit to soothe you. As your senses become sharper, you become hyper-aware, enabling you to see and perceive the wisdom and calmness within you.

June 17

Amor Fati

Acceptance of both self and others clarifies and compels appropriate action.

Few life skills are more valuable than the ability to accept yourself and others. Acceptance is not acquiescence. It is recognizing what is and is not to our liking and within our control. With that clarity, we then can decide whether and how best to respond.

The inability to accept oneself results in self-doubt and self-judgment, which can lead to underestimating or denigrating our abilities and strengths. It can also prompt us to put some people on false pedestals of admiration and others in the dark hole of disdain.

Grant yourself and others some grace. Make a concerted effort to accept yourself and others. You do not have to be satisfied or pleased, only accepting. Immerse yourself in the present without reminiscence of yesterday or apprehension of tomorrow. Avoid conditionalized acceptance: "I will be happy with myself when I am ___," or I will be happy with you when you are ___." That's like saying your journey will be complete when you reach the horizon; you will never reach the ever-present horizon and never be happy. Learn to accept yourself and others as you and they are now, without regard for what was yesterday or may be tomorrow.

June 18

Mortality
Live until you die.

It is a simple thought yet challenging in practice. Our world is created when we are born and exists as long as we do. In our youth, we look forward and see a vast uncharted landscape and presume we have an almost unlimited amount of time to live ... until we do not. As elders, we reflect on our life's mosaic and are disappointed to see so many voids created by squandered time. Time we could have spent living but chose merely to exist. Time marches relentlessly on, waiting for no one. It is up to each of us to choose whether we waste or maximize every moment of our lives. We never know when our time will run out, so we should not squander what is so precious.

Begin each day with a "live for today" mindset, a to-do list of what matters to you and enriches your life, and shed yourself of unwarranted burdens. Remember, it takes time for things to happen in an instant. Live until you die.

June 19

Emotion

Praise and blame, like good and evil, are the perspective of others.

We enjoy the ethereal feeling of praise and despise the sting of blame. We exert effort for one and ardently try to avoid the other. All the while, we forget that each of those is another person's perspective of our actions. Why do we give so much significance to someone else's opinion and so little to our own? Their opinion is a reflection of them, of the esteem with which they view themselves and measure others.

Critically and realistically, self-judge your effort. Celebrate yourself while you seek to improve yourself. Care what others say and think, but examine their assessment of you through your own lens and don't give it more weight than your own judgment. Be honest with yourself, and trust yourself.

June 20

Awareness

In solitude, we seek calm and self-awareness. In isolation, we seek escape and detachment from reality.

Solitude is a state of self-sufficiency. It is the ability to buffer external distractions and to self-soothe and self-examine. Solitude enables us to self-engage without disengaging from society and to be a part of society without being entirely dependent on it. Solitude involves a level of ease in being alone, even amidst a buzzing crowd in a crowded room. The sense of self-reliance and independence that solitude brings can be empowering and liberating.

Conversely, isolation is a state of self-denial. Isolation is a breeding ground for helplessness, inertia, and decline. It tends to deplete rather than restore, leading to a deepening sense of separation, loneliness, and helplessness that only perpetuates the cycle of isolation. Chronic isolation can slowly eat away at the mind, sinking the individual deeper and deeper into a pit of despair and potentially insanity.

While solitude fosters inner strength, isolation breeds debilitating despair. Avoid isolation, and seek professional help if you find yourself entrapped by it. Take time for solitude, a few moments or hours or days or whatever time you need to calm and reinforce yourself.

June 21

Social Thought

It is summer solstice; the daylight maximizes its dominance over dark. Wisdom illuminates both the lightness and darkness of life, enabling us to distinguish the difference.

Everything and everyone around you is a potential source of knowledge, providing insights about themselves and their experiences or you and yours. The question is, are you willing to learn?

Wisdom has inherent value and often comes from unexpected places and at unpredictable times. Trust the lessons of nature. Nature has no objectives or bias; it simply is, and therefore, its lessons are sound. Try to learn from others, regardless of the source or nature of their wisdom, knowing it is a reflection of their experiences and acquired knowledge. Be receptive, but exercise discernment; unlike nature, people may have self-motivated agendas.

A con artist can be as instructive as a sage; one informs us how not to be and the other how to be. It's up to you to discern the difference. Understanding others, nature, and oneself is critical to understanding life. Be a lifelong student and learn as you go, wisely choosing your direction and moving ever forward.

June 22

Action
Character is not inherent. It is created.

Character is not an essential nature a person is born with. Character is the sum of the characteristics a person displays to the world. These characteristics do not come naturally. They are learned. Character is built with the characteristics one chooses to develop. Character is a combination of body, mind, and soul, and it is unique to each person.

Your character is created by you, influenced by your environment and by how you view yourself, others, and life. Your character is reflected in your actions, especially when no one is watching. Everyone has the choice of being a person of poor character or virtuous character. Each day offers an opportunity to recognize and eliminate characteristics that diminish our character. Each day offers an opportunity to build, strengthen, and practice virtuous qualities.

Be mindful of your character and your resulting actions. Be aware of those who may wish to slander your character. Seek to enhance and protect your character, keeping the bigger picture in mind.

June 23

Problem Solving

We have the option of boldly stepping up or timidly stepping away, of acting courageously or relinquishing our power to act.

No one is born bold or timid. Both are characteristics that are developed and practiced. It is easier to be bold when you are physically, mentally, and spiritually prepared to face challenges and obstacles, regardless of origin. Being bold ensures you can play the cards you are dealt. Fear and anxiety result in timid behavior, which can bring scorn and put you in compromising positions. Being timid forces you to play the cards someone else deals you.

Developing your personal triad—your body, mind, soul—not only facilitates life balance, it also emboldens you to make tough choices and take difficult actions. Prepare for your life journey as a warrior, intellect, and sage. Be bold as you face the trials of life. Be bold but conscientious, not reckless. Be a model of calm strength and mindful leadership. Be a model for emulation.

June 24

Resilience

To forgive others, you must first forgive yourself; to be kind to others, you must first be kind to yourself. Benevolence begins with self-care.

Regardless of yesterday's events, the sun rises each morning, giving each of us a fresh start, without reservation. As citizens of the world, it is important to be supportive of others. But we are only responsible for ourselves, and at times we are our own worst critics. Maybe we should focus on caring for ourselves, first or at least commensurate with the care we give others. After all, there is nothing to share if the cup is empty.

Do for yourself what you do for others. Accept yourself as you would accept others. Forgive yourself as you would forgive others. Be kind to yourself as you would be kind to others. Give yourself quarter as you would give others theirs. Be both a facilitator and a model of self-care and of caring for others with grace.

June 25

Amor Fati

Forgiveness can be one of life's most difficult decisions and actions. It could also be lifesaving. Without forgiveness, the future is bleak.

Life is full of challenges. They distress, frustrate, and sometimes impede us, and so we work to avoid or overcome them. Each challenge makes us wiser and stronger, often in ways we do not immediately recognize. Forgiving someone absolutely and unconditionally for their transgressions is one of the most difficult challenges in life—surpassed only by the challenge of forgiving ourselves.

Without forgiveness, we risk being trapped in a cycle of revenge and retaliation, whether as individuals or as social groups. This death spiral inhibits progress and leads us deeper into despair, preventing understanding or compromise and leading to failure. As difficult as forgiveness may be, it is magical. It is powerful and transformative. It paves the way for a brighter future. Forgiveness has the potential to heal us, save our souls, and positively impact the lives of our children.

Believe in yourself, trust in others, and have the courage to forgive both.

June 26

Mortality

Once we acknowledge everyone's mortality, we can recognize our commonality and strive for better aspects of life.

There is something liberating in knowing we all share something. Sharing binds us and brings a level of commonality. If we allow ourselves to transcend the daily tussles, misunderstandings, and misrepresentations, we might embrace the fact that we all will eventually leave our physical form. If we can agree on that, this acknowledgment gives us the power to look past today's unsettling disturbances. It allows us to think and act with a broader perspective and deeper compassion.

There are those who will choose to use this awareness as an excuse to perpetuate hate and violence, falsely believing it does not matter what they do if we're all going to die anyway. Why not continue the callous bludgeoning of others to preserve their self-conceived superiority? Because their selfish actions perpetuate hate from generation to generation. We all die. It may be better if their unfounded egocentric ideas and beliefs died first.

June 27

Emotion

To love deeply means there will be deep grief.

We are creatures of emotion. No matter how much we try to use logic to guide our lives, we are still affected by emotion. Among the most impactful of our feelings is love. It fills and consumes us. It puts us at ease and unease. It makes us strong and vulnerable. More importantly, deep, passionate, unconditional love will result in deep grief when our loved one leaves us. The pain of our loss is exaggerated by our profound, soulful love for them. We must relish our moments as we travel our paths together. When our paths diverge, let's hold each other in our thoughts until our paths cross again.

June 28

Awareness

Listening and observing are powerful instruments of learning and understanding.

There is something to learn from everyone and everything around you. Every person and experience can teach you something about themselves and, more importantly, about you. Are you listening? Are you willing to learn from any source? Are you tuned into your surroundings? Are you paying attention to nature? Or are you plugged into your phone and distracted?

Few actions are more important than listening when others are sharing. Conversely, the least significant action is sharing when no one is listening. The probability of saying something foolish is proportional to how much you talk. The likelihood of hearing something important is proportional to how much you listen. Rather than listening passively and talking actively, we should be actively listening and passively talking. Only then will we position ourselves to learn when people and nature are desperately trying to teach us.

June 29

Social Thought

The most challenging adversary we face is ourselves.

Each of us is shaped by our beliefs, mindsets, knowledge, and experiences. As we go through life, we take in an enormous amount of input, which we must carefully parse. As changes occur, we must assess ourselves to determine whether, when, and how to pivot to ensure we're on the right path. When we fail to parse and pivot, we end up obstructing and battling ourselves.

Be aware that, if you allow, your associations can wield too much influence over your choices. If you begin to act like them, you will be judged like them and your future may be decided by them, so choose wisely. Be you. Think for yourself. And find your own way.

Amid the transitions along your journey, don't cling to mindsets and habits that no longer serve you. Adjust, adapt, and adopt new ways to manage your life. Whether you're being a friend or foe to yourself at the time, be honest with and kind to yourself. Take stock, take control, and take action to get back on track.

June 30

Action

Respect your opinions more than the opinions of others, and compromise from a position of strength.

People who are emotionally immature and insecure tend to value the opinions of others more than their own. By allowing reason to guide your life rather than extreme emotional swings, your experience and self-confidence will grow. With each analysis of an idea, opinion, or situation, both your knowledge and your self-respect will grow. You'll confidently make quick decisions based on experience, taking a moment to ensure they are driven by knowledge and direction, not by passion. If you find yourself needing to compromise, you can then do so from a position of strength rather than relying on others' thoughts and direction.

Strive to be self-aware, not self-absorbed. Remain open to, yet skeptical of, new or differing points of view, and critically analyze any supposed evidence or proof.

July

July 1

Problem Solving

Wisdom doesn't come from age; it comes from experiences. Study yields knowledge; learning comes from experience and the wise always have more to live, learn, and experience.

Being older or knowledgeable does not guarantee wisdom. Having wisdom involves accurately perceiving and appropriately responding to reality, not merely reading and hearing about it. A person can be well-read and well-educated, but lack in life experiences or the ability to learn from them.

Neither does maturity necessarily equate to wisdom. Elders do not hold a monopoly on wisdom simply because they've lived longer, nor are youngsters wise beyond their years with so many still ahead of them. Whether you're 80 or 18, age is insignificant if you have yet to live a full life and learn from it. Just because I'm older doesn't mean I'm wiser.

Regardless of your age and how wise you are today, acquiring wisdom is an ongoing process. Live fully. Keep learning. Grow wiser through living what you've learned.

July 2

Resilience

It isn't religion or intellect that gets us through terrible times; it is a calm and steady mind.

The ability to keep calm and think straight steals strength from misfortune and stymies your enemies. An unthinking or tormented mind, especially in challenging times, is like an angry ocean, roaring and crashing inside you, driven by a lashing wind. Calm your mind and let the tempest subside to regain your composure, then you can face hardship with more stability.

An intellectually curious mind can be at odds with a calm, quiet one. One pushes for answers by leaning into chaos; the other offers solutions through quiet reflection. We need both in equal parts. There is a time for the assessment and disruption of intellectual curiosity—but that time is not in the face of a storm. Steal the strength of misfortune and the energy of your tormentors by staying calm. Sound actions will be your reward.

July 3

Amor Fati

It is not possible to be both egocentric and altruistic. It is possible and beneficial to be both self-aware and aware of others.

When you stand before a window and gaze out, do you find yourself searching for the reflection of your image or for a broader view of the outside world? It is human nature to seek both views, the internal and external. You always have a choice whether to direct your focus toward introspection and self-analysis or toward understanding and interacting with the world. Humans are social animals with strong self-awareness, which can lead to self-centeredness. Egotistical people are led by their vanity, which dominates their every thought and action. They don't look beyond themselves to see or consider anyone or anything that doesn't serve them.

We are each part of the incredible world around us. If we forget we are a piece of the world's mosaic and think the world revolves and relies upon us, we are lost souls. When you see your image as a part of the greater view, you become part of something amazing. The possibilities become almost endless when we work together rather than in isolation.

July 4

Mortality

All living things rise and fall, advance and retreat.

Watching a child grow is the inverse of watching a senior's decline. A child rises and advances, often at an astounding pace. A senior falls and retreats, sometimes slowly and other times quickly. One is thrilling, the other sad; both are critical aspects of life.

As adults in the long gap between childhood and the elder years, we strive to improve and yet do not prepare for the precipice of decline. Although we often instinctively sense a potential fall, we don't often predict its magnitude. Rarely are we prepared for the decline and limitations of our aging bodies and minds.

Here's how you can prepare for what everyone must someday face: First, acknowledge and accept its inevitability, whether sooner or later. Then, to ease the fall, face the known and unknown with the same eager open mind, without prejudice and preconceived end. Focus on what you can do, rather than on what you can't. Regardless of your knowledge and experience, approach everything with the eyes of youth, of a beginner, eager to learn and experience new things.

July 5

Emotion

When we succumb to our emotions, we lose control of our destiny.

Do you possess the emotional awareness to understand your feelings and the maturity to express them calmly? If yes, your emotions can be used to your advantage. If not, they could lead to your downfall.

Some people use their emotions, overtly or covertly, to provoke strong emotions, like anger, fear, elation, or hope in others, as a power play for control. This emotional manipulation is intended to deceive, humiliate, punish, or simply create a scene. When your emotions run hot and high, they can override your thoughts and behaviors. That not only puts you at the mercy of emotional manipulators, it also puts you at risk of sabotaging yourself. Recognize and see through the charade, use their theatrics to your advantage and don't allow yourself to play along. Nothing disarms an emotional inciter better than failing to light the flame.

Bear in mind, emotional states are as infectious as physical diseases. You can suffer from another person's uncontrolled emotions just as much as suffering from your own. Deflate irrational emotional outbursts, yours and others, with a sharp and steady mind.

July 6

Awareness

Looking back at what was or might have been or forward to what may or may not be, can blind us to what we can experience and contribute today.

The future transforms into the present, which soon becomes the past, all in their own time, not ours. Our past experiences inform our actions today, which shape our future. Today, we can look back with regret or gratitude, or we can look forward with anxiety or hope, or we can look for opportunities to improve and grow, to experience and enjoy life, to be kind, compassionate, tolerant, and understanding. These are our choices, your choices, every moment of every day. Don't let the past or future cast a shadow over today. Go do something for yourself, for others, for the world.

July 7

Social Thought

It is harder to create value than to earn money. Value is enduring; money is transient.

Creating value drives progress, makes lasting impacts, and infuses one generation's ideas, ideals, and aspirations into another. Earning money is a transactional, necessary part of life and business, which results in short-term goal attainment. Value is esoteric; money is tangible. Both are essential.

Unfortunately, we are more often judged by the money we amass than the value we create. Our "value" in society is measured by what we have earned. Financial wealth and status end when you die, but created value lives on. Value creators are the unsung heroes of today and champions of tomorrow. They create something much more important and long-lasting than money. Creating value enriches life in meaningful, if not material, ways—for both the value creator and those they impact.

Perhaps we should strive less to earn money and more to create value, or at least put equal effort into creating value and earning money. Perhaps the value we create can be our legacy, the measure by which future generations evaluate our contribution.

July 8

Action

We are accountable for our words and actions, for which we shouldn't blame or credit others.

Imagine being at the helm of a boat on a misty river as another boat advances toward you. You scream and yell for the craft to alter course, with no results ... until there is a collision and you discover the vessel was adrift. Rather than yelling for others to change course, instead you could alter yours, avoid the collision, and continue on your way. Your misfortunes are yours to bear because most were yours to avoid.

That said, some misfortunes are unavoidable, including those perpetrated by someone with ill intent. Even then, it's still up to you to take control and manage the best you can. If someone else's misdeeds throw you off course, do not wish for or seek conflict or calamities with or for them. You have new challenges to face that must be met with integrity and humility.

Take control of yourself as well as the situation, regardless of how or by whom it was originated or played out. Do what you can, and do not rely on anyone else's actions.

July 9

Problem Solving

Self-knowledge empowers and frees us to recognize and create solutions.

Those who advance themselves physically, mentally, or spiritually continuously challenge themselves. They are constantly probing, trying to find and extend their limits and purposely putting themselves in uncomfortable situations. These exceptional individuals seek to understand the unknown both around them and within themselves. They know part of attaining a goal is in the struggle. Practicing the fundamentals forges your saber from raw steel. The heat, sweat, and every hammer blow of failure and success create something unique; they create you.

Contemplate uncertainty and the unknown, especially within yourself and your discomfort. Seek to understand yourself as much as you seek to understand the unknown around you. Dig deep, reach high, and do the hard, steady work of forging ahead.

July 10

Resilience

Surviving failure with dignity and acknowledging success with humility builds resilience.

We gain strength from accepting defeat and moving on, and we lose strength from denying or clinging to our failure. We also gain strength from recognizing how we and others contribute to success, and we lose strength and focus by sitting back and basking in our glory. Resilience comes from being accountable for what goes both well and poorly in our lives.

Resist the temptation to deny responsibility for either positive or negative outcomes. Openly and graciously give credit where earned, to others and yourself, with integrity and humility. Accept fault, whether yours or others, and blame neither. Reflect on the events, analyze what went wrong and right, and consider how to improve, dwelling on neither outcome. Remember, you can't change the past, but you can change how you react to and approach similar situations in the future. Embrace experience, whether triumph or defeat—as a step along your path for greater learning and expanded growth.

July 11

Amor Fati
Life's events change our focus. Our focus changes our lives.

The course of our lives can change at any bend. Just as a river changes more in turbulent waters, so do the troubled waters of life change us. Change also emerges from still water, for in tranquility we reflect, see possibilities for change, and build up our reserves to change. Turbulence forces change; tranquility fosters change. Either way, our body, mind, and spirit shift into sharp focus, enabling us to better adapt to life's changes or to better affect change in our lives.

We run into trouble when we drift into stasis, unwilling or unable to change. Stasis is unnatural, for it is the nature of all things to change. Statis leads to stagnation, which cannot sustain much less enrich life.

Live with a focused purpose, whether it be pleasure, passion, work, or enlightenment. Focus, and be ready and willing to change to survive and thrive.

July 12

Mortality
Why fill life with have-to-dos when life offers so many get-to-dos?

Is your life an unending list of things you *have to do*, or replete with things you *get to do*? Examine your obligations and ask why you are a slave to them. A change of perspective is all it takes. Even the routine can be meaningful and enjoyable. There may also be new things to experience. Our lives are full of things we get to do.

This perspective becomes especially important when thinking about your mortality. It might motivate you to increase your get-to-dos. It may encourage you to be more present in everything you get to do. It may make you appreciate it more, wondering if it's the last time you get to do it. When family members and friends pass away, you will be comforted by the memories of the get-to-dos you shared with them.

You get one life, and you get to decide whether to fill it with burdens or opportunities. Eliminate the have-to-dos and fill your life with as many get-to-dos as possible. When you get to do something, make the most of it.

July 13

Emotion

We diminish our ability to support others and ourselves when we allow ourselves to be pulled into the emotional whirlpools of others.

People may unintentionally or intentionally pull you into their emotional dramas. While being empathetic enables you to understand and support others, it is critical to establish boundaries, lest you get sucked into their emotional whirlpools. When you get carried away by another person's emotional turmoil, you can lose sight of both your effectiveness in the situation and your goals and priorities.

Learning to identify when you are being pulled into these emotional vortexes allows you to take a step back and assess the situation objectively. Knowing your boundaries—how much you can engage without compromising yourself—enables you to disengage and move on.

By moving on, you consciously decide to focus on what you can control and influence. This protects your emotional and mental health. It enables you to approach challenges with a clear and calm mind. It also empowers you to invest your valuable time and energy into relationships and experiences that enrich your life and contribute to your personal growth.

July 14

Awareness

Be objectively observant to see clearly in chaos.

It is fine to have prolonged periods of silence and doubt in conversations and dealings with others. Although silent pauses are uncomfortable for most people, they provide an opportunity to observe, think, and study before speaking or committing.

Hold your silence and your opinions to gather the information you need, and never doubt yourself while asking why and how, thus keeping your mental freedom. Do not be afraid of or avoid the truth simply because it is unpleasant; face it and embrace it for what it is. The safest place is the most dangerous: It is when you let your guard down and relax, assuming nothing can harm you except your lack of awareness. Try to be dispassionately observant and to not let down your guard or your sense of awareness. It is your clear and keen eyes and ears that will discern deceit and danger in a chaotic world.

July 15

Social Thought
Time wasted is life lost.

Time is unseen and unfelt, yet it is both finite and infinite. We lose time due to distractions, ignorance, and a lack of focus and knowledge. We get caught up in petty issues simply because they are small and we can resolve them. We waste precious time because we are unwilling to search for the whole truth and broad knowledge. We let ourselves spin around aimlessly because we have little or no direction. We recognize the value of time with loved ones just before their death, but squander so much of it during their lives.

Pay attention to what consumes your time. Anything that isn't worth your time is a waste of your time. Anything that is necessary to and/or brings value to your life is well spent time. Focusing on one thing at a time usually makes better use of your time than multitasking. So does walking away when bored, tired, or frustrated. Release, relax, and refresh to regroup. Spend time with your thoughts and on self-care; they allow you to recharge and refocus.

July 16

Action

Aspirations are hindered by fear and facilitated by conviction.

The first step in decreasing fear and increasing confidence is to recognize both what you fear and what gives you confidence. You can neither stop nor capitalize on what you don't acknowledge. Remove obstacles by facing and pushing past your fear and toward your aspirations. Strengthen your resolve by pressing forward with your strengths—the knowledge, skills, mindsets, and focus your command. Lean into your strengths to overcome your uncharted boundaries. After all, they are arbitrary and self-imposed. Activate your strengths to fuel your conviction and move you forward.

Be self-aware enough to honestly take the blame for your part in any failure. Blaming others diminishes your ability to improve. Be self-aware enough to believe in yourself and your aspirations. Everything is possible when you commit yourself to your dreams, no matter how bold. Solutions to challenges appear when you remove the veil of fear and doubt. Progress is made when you lean into your strengths and lead with your heart, muscling onward while keeping your eye on the dream. Never Fear The Dream.

July 17

Problem Solving

Motivate others by touching their emotions, dreams, and fears, and you will have moved them from their core.

A motivated leader leads by example. A motivational leader leads by example *and* by touching the hearts and souls of those they aspire to lead. We can learn from and be motivated by both, but their approaches differ and their potential impact on us can differ greatly.

The most enthusiastic, motivated leaders may sway people to do great things or only the minimum required. The most effective, motivational leaders may inspire and guide people to improve or transform themselves and their lives. With a motivational leader, your cause spiritually becomes theirs. They are yours to command and will perform acts beyond the norm, just because they believe in your dream. This is an enormous power.

Choose your motivated leaders or motivational leaders wisely, and proceed with awareness. If they use their power justly, they can help you get through a rough patch or improve yourself and your life. If they abuse their power, their zealous passion can sweep you aside.

July 18

Resilience

Only with awareness of both our vulnerabilities and dependencies can we maximize our abilities and alliances.

We all have vulnerabilities and dependencies. Both are usually viewed as and can be disadvantages, but they can also work to our advantage. Empathy, for example, can be a vulnerability that overrides reason; it can also enable us to be more perceptive, understanding, and effective. While reliance on someone or something can constrain us, a win-win interdependency can result in a strong interlinked team.

Be aware of your vulnerabilities and dependencies as well as how you view and handle them. Recognize when your vulnerabilities have become excuses are limiting you and when you've become overly dependent upon people, organizations, or things. Do not enslave yourself to your own trappings. Do not be enslaved by warrantless obligations, narcissists, or the greedy. See your vulnerabilities and dependencies for what they are. Adjust your perspectives and employ your abilities to achieve the objective and the advantage of all involved, including yourself. In so doing, you take away the dark power of self-sabotage and of those who hobble or block you. You empower yourself.

July 19

Amor Fati

Your level-headed assessment of yourself matters far more than the transient opinions of others.

Never read, much less believe, your own press. Extravagant platitudes and biting criticisms tend to reflect more about the people expressing them than you. Such zealous external opinions are often expressed by those who are envious of or oppose you, either as a means to manipulate how others perceive you, or how you see yourself and react to these opinions, or both. If you allow them any credibility, your ego will see condemnation as oppressive and applause as liberating; both are dangerous.

Let your sense of self and your progress be guided by your values, efforts, and motivations rather than by the fluctuating praise or condemnation from the outside world. Consider what others think of you, but don't give their opinions too much weight or be blind to their ulterior motives. Absorb their cheering platitudes and piercing criticisms with the same disdain. Honestly assess your goals, ideas, actions, and progress, but don't be too easy or too hard on yourself. Self-criticism is beneficial, but self-congratulation can lead to complacency, and self-flagellation is destructive.

July 20

Mortality

Forgiveness releases the past and liberates the future.

What are you waiting for? Make peace within yourself and then with others. Regardless of who threw the first stone or delivered the harshest blow, is holding a grudge worth the relentless pain and suffering it causes? We start with nothing and end with nothing. In between, we complicate our lives with intoxicating and egotistical opinions, emotions, and actions, only to end our lives boxed in by infirmities and senility.

Keep life simple. It eases the struggle as we live and the depression as we falter. Resolve the unresolved today. Why wait until your deathbed to let go of the burdens you carry and embrace what gives your life meaning? Forgive yourself and others. Make amends when you can, and find peace within.

July 21

Emotion

No one is entitled to privilege, and no one deserves oppression. Everyone has the right to justice and a responsibility to themselves and society.

People accustomed to living a privileged life often feel superior and entitled to their privileges. People accustomed to living under oppression often feel unjustly judged as inferior, exploited by the privileged, and deprived of privilege. The privileged tend to resist equality. The oppressed tend to demand equality. When those opposing forces build potency and collide, the world becomes consumed with anger, jealousy, and defensiveness—three of the most vile and powerful of human emotions. The inevitable outcomes are discord, divisiveness, deficiency, and destruction.

No one has the right to withhold and covet basic human rights and privileges. Everyone has an obligation to treat everyone else with respect. No one is or is not entitled. Everyone has the right to reap life's riches and the responsibility to do their part to ensure the greater good. Be introspective and ask yourself: What would I do if I were on the other side? If you are being honest, you would relax your grip on privileges or unclench your fist of demand.

July 22

Awareness

Set and survey your course. Live and relish your journey.

While trekking life's trail, stay clear-headed and observant. Acknowledge what is around you without losing sight of your ultimate destination. Keep your head up and your senses alert. It's hard to look ahead when you're looking down at your next step. Every moment brings new circumstances, which can throw obstacles or opportunities in your path. Challenge yourself to bravely face and wisely use both.

If you want to travel far in life, strive to make consistent progress while enjoying the journey. Find humor along the way, even in the most trying circumstances, even if it's laughing at yourself; your journey will be much more pleasant for you and others. Whatever your path, commit to it and be true to it.

July 23

Social Thought

Noise creates distraction and illusion. Silence enhances focus and clarity.

Be comfortable in silence, relishing all the things you hear and see around you, especially those you are experiencing for the first time. Withhold your concurrence or rejection until you fully understand other people's ideas or opinions. Be wary of and refrain from immediately responding to those who have too much to say about too many topics. This could signify their insecurity and/or ignorance cloaked in a blanket of pontification and bluster. Assess their depth of knowledge and perspective from a basis of facts, not emotions. Those who are jabberers often have little evidence to support their voluminous comments and self-serving motives.

July 24

Action

Knowledge without practice is theoretical and limiting. Applied knowledge is tangible and liberating.

If all you do is study and never take action to utilize what you've learned, you will never fully understand or benefit from your studies. Your academic prowess is tested only when you close the books and implement what you've learned. Real learning stems from education and training combined with life experiences that put your studies to the test. No matter how much you study and learn from your studies, only by applying it can you expand your knowledge and learn from both your successes and failures.

Put your studies into practice. Be prepared for the bruises of failure and the bittersweet taste of success. Learn from your experiences, and grow your wisdom. Your academic awards and diplomas mean you have demonstrated a capacity to learn.

July 25

Problem Solving

Deceit and distractions exacerbate problems. Open-minded, even-tempered assessment solves problems.

To focus on the merits and facts of an issue, we must be willing to question our own beliefs and motives just as critically as we challenge the motives and beliefs of others. Those who care only about themselves often use actions and words to distract and deceive us. By the same token, we can distract and deceive ourselves by refusing or neglecting to examine our ideas, opinions, and emotions.

Avoid being distracted by shiny baubles, flattering words, or exaggerated declarations, all of which are just distractions. When any of these arise, be cautious of falsehoods and deception. Try to uncover the other person's or organization's underlying point of view and motives. Take a hard look at your mindsets, opinions, and emotions surrounding a problem or situation. Be prepared to explain and defend your position, but consider all positions. Focus on resolving the issue, calmly and objectively, based on the facts, demerits, and merits associated with the issue.

July 26

Resilience

The power to withstand life's storms lies in the eye of calm within, which precedes and directs action.

There will be times of strife and discomfort in your life that might prompt you to take immediate action. But do you have to act? Do you really? Now? Sometimes, the more powerful act is to do nothing.

Fear of something bad happening or of not getting or of losing something you want or value exaggerates perceived danger or loss, which can trigger anger or anxiety, which can drive you into rash action. When you give yourself a chance to dial down the emotions and assess the situation *before* you act, it is easier to navigate your way through challenges.

Every obstacle is an opportunity to learn and to grow stronger mentally, physically, and emotionally. Don't squander these amazing circumstances. Regardless of the unfortunate nature of the event, look past the strife, learn from it, find some humor in it, and grow. You will be better prepared to take appropriate action and move forward.

July 27

Amor Fati

The body is an instrument of the mind. The mind is a conduit of the soul. The soul is the pilot and power of our physical and intellectual being.

Why do we allow our bodies to become a representation of who we are, what we are capable of, and how we are perceived? While the body is a critical aspect of each person's personal triad—body, mind, soul—it should never be the key driver of our lives. Having a strong, healthy body to carry and interact with our mind is important. However, the world is filled with geniuses who have physical disabilities as well as physically fit people who have intellectual or mental health challenges. Yet, we are often judged and judge ourselves by our physical appearances, rather than who we are.

Who you are is your soul, manifested in your body and mind. Let your soul shine through. Embrace the physical, mental, and spiritual aspects of your being. Always keep this thought in the forefront: a strong body and mind remain an empty vessel until filled with spiritual understanding and peace. Be defined as a whole person, a complete triad of body, mind, soul.

July 28

Mortality

Each spiritual path is unique to the individual and nobody's business.

It is condescending for anyone to claim their religion or spiritual path is superior and reprehensible to condemn others for not subscribing to their beliefs. No one has the right to belittle another person's religious or spiritual path. Everyone has the right to discover and follow their own path. Embrace and exercise your religious or spiritual beliefs and practices, but don't impose them upon others. Respect the spiritual paths of others without judgment, even if you don't understand, agree with, or like their beliefs. Be glad for whatever comfort and direction their spirituality brings them.

Some people follow a religion to give them peace from fear. Others follow a spiritual path to give them peace within themselves. Throughout your life's journey, seek enlightenment and eschew rhetoric. Seek peace within, and strive to live righteously. Let your life reflect your spirit.

July 29

Emotion

The struggle between good and evil is waged every day within each of us.

Good and evil exist and have a place in our world, on that most of us agree. Where we differ is in our perception of evil and good and the blurred boundary between them. Instead of scrutinizing the good versus evil conflict in the world, pay more attention to your internal struggle to discern between good and evil. Resolve what is good and evil and to what degree within yourself, and let others do the same. We may never agree upon the shades between good and evil. However, we can accept that few things in life are absolutely good or absolutely evil. Abject evil will be called out by everyone except those using it for their benefit. Greater good will be recognized by everyone except those whose perceptions blind them to it. What matters is that we, individually and collectively, strive to recognize and live within the margins of good.

July 30

Awareness

There is no need to shout if someone is listening.

People yell for various reasons: to get or divert attention, out of frustration or desperation, in anger or fear, or simply to be heard because no one seems to be listening.

Listening is essential to all communication. Yet, it is one of the most challenging skills to master, and few know how to listen. Being an active listener requires remaining silent while others are speaking and focusing on what they are saying. Instead, we too often half-listen, so caught up in formulating our retorts that we hear only snippets of what the speaker is saying or interrupt before they've finished articulating their idea. Conversations degrade into yelling matches, with each side presenting their view without trying to understand the other's.

If you ever find yourself raising your voice, take a moment to assess the situation. Is no one listening? Or are you just venting? Speak firmly and with conviction, and avoid shouting, which is more apt to close minds than open them. Listen attentively to understand. You might be surprised by how much common ground exists.

July 31

Social Thought

An ill-directed mind inflicts more significant harm than any hater or enemy. The collective mind of the mob is a conglomerate of ill-directed minds wreaking havoc.

Our own misguided thoughts, attitudes, and prejudices can do substantial damage to self and society. When a group of people latch on to the same or similar ill-guided thoughts, attitudes, and/or prejudices, the chaos created and the damage done are exponentially worse.

Guard yourself against the irrational, misdirected minds of an uncontrollable mob—its individual members engaging in self-destruction while creating mass confusion and hysteria in a collective hive of ruin. Your ability to think clearly, manage your emotions, and resist the harmful misguidance of group dynamics will give you the direction you need to chart your own course. When you think for and control yourself, you are in a better position to minimize self-sabotaging thoughts, emotions, and actions, ultimately preventing self-defeat and strengthening your self-control.

August

August 1

Action

Some people push for change; others push against it. Leaders initiate and manage change.

Change, by its very nature, is challenging for most people. It creates uncertainty and often requires adjustments that many are hesitant to make. Most individuals do not actively pursue change; many are reluctant to accept change when it inevitably occurs. The willingness and ability to embrace and manage change is a beneficial life skill.

Pursue change and act on it, but don't push it on others. Instead, seek to understand why they are reluctant to the change, and explain how it may and may not affect them. To ease their perceived pain and suffering associated with change, find a way to link it to accepted practices of the past. Drawing connections between the new and the old can create a sense of familiarity and continuity. This can make the transition smoother and more palatable for those who are resistant. Change built on something familiar, valued, and trusted will be seen as something to consider, trust, and accept.

August 2

Problem Solving

In times of crises, those of higher character take the higher ground and have the upper hand.

A crisis can bring out the best and worst in people, especially leaders. Among the worst are scapegoating, demagoguery, and dishonesty. Guard yourself against those who blame and castigate others; who exploit the fears, prejudices, ignorance, and hatred of others; who disseminate misinformation and lies. Do not fear or be fooled by those who bully, undermine, and dominate others and who favor the select few and discriminate against others, including minorities and the disadvantaged.

During any crisis, regardless of magnitude, protect your character and reputation by recognizing and rejecting these low-character traits, loudly and resolutely. If you find yourself getting swept up into someone else's tirades, take stock of whether their beliefs and behaviors align with yours. Consider that whatever "wins" they gain through their malicious, manipulative tactics are undeserved and untenable, and their poor character and ill intent will eventually be exposed.

August 3

Resilience

The more one knows the more one knows they don't know.

While the unknown is limitless, our knowledge has limits. As our knowledge increases, so does our awareness of more and the greater unknown. Imagine drawing a small circle. The area within represents your current knowledge. It is what you know. The area outside is limitless and represents the unknown. It is what you don't know. Therefore, the circumference of the circle represents the connection between the known and unknown. As we grow and learn, our circle of knowledge increases and the area of our circle gets bigger. But so does the circumference, our recognition that there is even more we don't know.

Continue to study, learn, and experience life and keep pressing your circle of knowledge. Grow the area of your knowledge with thirst and hunger. Embrace the new understanding and thrill of knowing there is always more to know and more you don't know.

August 4

Amor Fati
You will go faster alone, but you will go further with help.

There are those among us who believe they are independent and don't need anyone's help. They believe they are nimbler and quicker without the burden of others slowing them. In some regards they may be right; however, an individual's capabilities are limited to themselves, and as such, their journey will have limits.

Conversely, a team learns from and supports the members of the team, each bringing their unique talents and expertise to support the journey of the team. The team may go slower but they will go further. There is no lead or lag in a team.

Everyone has strengths and weaknesses. We are each better at some things than others. We can also improve through our intention, study, practice, and sometimes with help from our friends, family, colleagues, and mentors. And everyone has something to offer. Yield to the strength within the team without the burden of ego. Give with humility. Receive with gratitude. Either way, you and everyone else are better together as we all advance on our journey.

August 5

Mortality

Life becomes too short only when we deprive ourselves of the time to live fully.

Just as *Lap Around the Sun* is of a fixed duration, so is your life span. The difference is that you know the number of pages in this book and the time for the Earth to circle the sun, but not the number of days in your life. When you live with intention, endeavoring to spend your time engaged in and experiencing what gives your life meaning, you'll have few, if any, regrets at the end of your life, even if it is shorter than desired. As important, you will relish the life you are living now. Strive to fill your days with as much love, wonder, and joy as you can. Take time to reflect, rest, and rejuvenate as you turn to look forward. Live purposefully, day by day.

August 6

Emotion

Justice is an empty promise when injustice goes unchallenged and unrectified.

Justice, the concept of being treated impartially and equitably, has been a virtuous pursuit for centuries. Yet, justice for all has yet to be achieved, primarily because it depends on who is on the receiving end of injustice.

When we feel violated, our sense of justice runs bone deep, compelling us to seek equity and retribution with an almost primal intensity. Our sense of justice tends to run skin deep when we don't recognize the injustice. Even when we finally acknowledge and abhor the injustice, we often do nothing or not enough to correct it. Then there are those who demand justice for themselves but think they can get away with violating others, revealing their self-serving perception of justice.

This dichotomy illustrates the complex duality of human morality and highlights the contrast between our ideals and actions. It serves as a poignant reminder that true justice requires consistency and integrity, not only when we are the victims but also when we hold the power to wrong others, whether with our actions or inactions.

August 7

Awareness

Our individual experiences represent a small fraction of the world's entirety but heavily influence our perception of it.

Make space in your perspective for the experiences of other people in the world. Your experiences and the knowledge you gained from them are an aspect of, but not the default or the center of, the whole human experience. Your experiences are critical to you and maybe those closest to you. Beyond that small circle, your experiences become a tiny part of the collective human experience and the knowledge gained from it, which grows exponentially over time. Everyone's experiences are just as meaningful as yours. Together, they continuously add to the sum of all human experiences, perspectives, and knowledge. Seek them, learn from them, and share them, as they are humankind's history and guides for tomorrow.

August 8

Social Thought
Mercy and wisdom are stronger than tradition.

The great prophets and the humanitarians embraced and socialized with those on the fringe of society. Rather than chastise or ridicule those of lesser means or status, they showed the strength of understanding and mercy. In their compassion and wisdom, they rejected religious traditions and social norms, rebelling against and ridiculing those who made a show of their piety, self-declared superiority, and hypocrisy. These people lived and risked their lives with a deep appreciation that regardless of social norms, we must look past our own ignorance, self-interest, and preconceived beliefs, for the betterment of all.

These leaders were examples for all of us to follow today. Each of us can objectively and respectfully challenge the validity of long-held traditions and accepted norms. The fringes of society remain a part of our social structure. Some may consider them the horsehair of our gold and silver brocade, but it is the base thread that binds all of us, regardless of how coarse. Exercise your wisdom and show your mercy to all, every day, regardless of tradition.

August 9

Action

Shortcuts have a propensity to sabotage rather than facilitate success.

Success cannot be achieved by taking shortcuts or the easy way out. Success requires unwavering perseverance over whatever period of time it takes to solve the problem, complete the task, or achieve the goal. That requires dedication, patience, resilience, and a relentless drive to keep pushing forward despite challenges.

Focus on the end goal and the fundamentals, emphasizing them at every step along the way. Early, subtle corrections are always preferable to drastic, late ones, which can be more difficult and time-consuming to implement. A well-defined vision combined with robust determination and an unyielding spirit has the incredible power to overcome any obstacle or challenge that comes your way, no matter how daunting it may seem. The key to success lies in the consistent and deliberate effort to improve and excel in every aspect of your endeavor.

August 10

Problem Solving
If you want peace, talk with your enemies, not your allies.

It is a simple concept: resolve issues with the people with whom you have the conflict, not anyone else. Your adversaries will likely be transparent, while those who present themselves as allies will be anything but. You will know where your opponent stands by their metaphorical fists raised in front of you, but you should have doubts about those behind you who may have hidden agendas.

Only through a one-on-one dialog with your opponent will either of you really understand the other's respective position. Both of you will inevitably harden your stances and may become louder and more animated. Your allies will inevitably appear to rally behind you with unsupported words of unyielding support. But if you falter, they may come to your aid only if it is in their best interest. You are their best friend, until you aren't. Pursue peace directly with your adversary, and be wary of the council of others.

August 11

Resilience

Self-liberation comes when we free ourselves from the chains of intolerance by expanding our knowledge and understanding.

No one is born a bigot, inherently programmed to condemn and oppress those who look, believe, worship, and live differently than they do. Bigotry, in all its manifestations, is taught, modeled, and learned. As we grow and are presented with new facts, experiences, and perspectives, we have the opportunity to reconsider what we've learned, consider new ideas and opinions, and adjust ours. Unfortunately, some people reject evidence that does not support their bigotry and then try to recruit others to blindly follow their way of thinking.

Each of us has the ability to discover what is right and wrong for ourselves. This can only be accomplished by expanding your knowledge and understanding, and thinking critically. Be wary of people who cling to their prejudices despite evidence to the contrary. Don't allow their passionate hate to distract you from your own sense of humanity. Use your intellect and experiences to form your own beliefs. Let your conscience be your guide.

August 12

Amor Fati

Acknowledging our capabilities and our limitations enables us to determine and forge the path forward.

Your current conditions and limitations are what they are. Embracing them for what they are doesn't mean accepting them as permanent constraints, defining you forever. Growth is a continuous and evolving process that requires time, patience, and dedication. Avoid fantasizing about capabilities you may never achieve, as this can lead to frustration and disappointment. Instead, realistically assess your present strengths and the resources currently at your disposal, and focus on using them to their fullest potential. Doing so lets you strategically and progressively overcome your limitations and achieve your goals.

Success is not an overnight accomplishment, but rather the result of realistic goal-setting, persistent effort, and a continuous commitment to self-improvement. Stay committed to your journey, understanding that every small step forward is part of a more significant path toward excellence.

August 13

Mortality

Life is too precious and too short for frivolous conflict.

Many people avoid settling quarrels and hold on to grudges, giving little or no thought to the reality that everyone has an expiration date that could come without warning or sooner than anticipated. The ability to acknowledge our own and everyone else's mortality gives us a unique perspective on life. Imagine having a bird's eye view of your life over time, with which you can observe people and events from a broad perspective. You'd be able to see how everything affects everything else. You'd be able to understand that the conflicts which seem so important are not. Given this grand perspective, you would realize the value of settling arguments amicably and peacefully.

August 14

Emotion

Anger proliferates conflict. Composure facilitates resolution.

Anger can be a beneficial emotion, for example, when it spurs us to demand justice, protect ourselves or others, or achieve a goal. This so-called "healthy" anger results in passionate and assertive behavior; it is a controlled and constructive emotion. "Toxic" anger results in aggressive, suppressive, or passive-aggressive behavior meant to intimidate or harm others; it is an uncontrolled and destructive emotion.

If, in the heat of an infuriating situation, your anger starts to rise or suddenly ignites, take a deep breath and try to calm yourself. If you can't find your calm, quietly remove yourself from the situation. Dousing another person's anger with your anger only yields a raging bonfire—consuming reason, compassion, and resolution in its flames. Conserve your energy for the far more constructive efforts of understanding and managing your emotions. In this chaotic world, strive to be a strong voice of calm reason and a fervent agent of peaceful resolution.

August 15

Awareness

A life without aspirations and goals is like a powerless, rudderless boat set adrift.

Except for humans, creatures of nature seem to have only primal goals of survival and procreation. Nature appears to be —devoid of objectives. The ocean and wind have no intentions; they just are. Yet, every wave and every gust yields a result. One thing that separates humans from other species is our ability to set long-term goals, express our aspirations, and have dreams of our future. Everyone has ambitions and is driven by them. We should have a clear sense of our goals, parse them into manageable steps, and detail a series of strategies, tactics, and actions (in that order) for achieving our goals.

Those without goals and aspirations tend to flounder, to pass their days squandering time and becoming more disillusioned. Consciously, without fear or trepidation, set bodacious goals for yourself. However, during this process know that success and failure are inevitable. Be humble with your victories, and learn from your defeats.

August 16

Social Thought

It is dangerous to put our faith and trust in something or someone that demands blind allegiance and rebukes independent thought.

Beware of those who seek or demand your absolute trust in, commitment to, and compliance with their teachings, beliefs, goals, tactics, or institutions. People of this ilk cannot be controlled by you or anyone else, nor are they influenced by norms, rules, laws, reason, or compassion. Their charade in pursuit of your trust will eventually be exposed for what it is: a ploy to advance themselves, not you. Do not become dependent on anyone or any organization that has faith only in itself. They do not deserve your discipleship. Have faith in the only thing you can control: yourself.

August 17

Action

Fears of boldness are disproportionate to reality, while the consequences of timidity are worse than imagined.

Boldness and timidity are learned behaviors. Fear of boldness can lead to timidity, while fear of timidity may push us toward boldness. These fears are often exaggerated mental constructs, not reflections of reality. That said, pervasive timidity can lead to missed opportunities, marginalization, and regret. Excessive boldness can lead to overconfidence, perceived arrogance, and mistrust. However, when the challenges are robust, or the stakes are high, you'll need boldness to break down barriers, open doors, and propel you forward.

It is possible to be introverted without being passive, and it is possible to be assertive without being abrasive. The process of developing and effectively utilizing boldness is gradual, involving small steps that challenge your fears and actions. Consistently choosing boldness in adversity can transform your personality and lead to a more empowered life. Even if it feels like a facade at first, boldness can eliminate doubts and reduce internal and external awkwardness.

August 18

Problem Solving

When we are focused on improving ourselves, our focus cannot be distracted by criticizing others or their criticisms of us.

Why are so many people so worried about what others do or don't do? Why do they look for and point out the shortcomings and faults of others? Is it because they fear others will criticize them? What a waste of time and energy it is to point out the flaws in others when no one knows another person's journey and we all have plenty of work to do on ourselves.

When we are focused on looking inward, addressing our own weaknesses, and utilizing our strengths, we don't have the time, energy, or desire to scrutinize and disparage others. Defaming others never looks good or works well for anyone in the long term.

Don't waste your life judging others or their choices. Focus on your decisions, actions, and motivations. Acknowledge, learn from, and correct your missteps and mistakes. Take criticism for what it is: an ill-informed opinion. Be proud of what you've done, and look forward to the things you will accomplish.

August 19

Resilience

In this world of invasive overexposure, be consistently inconsistent; master the art of modulation.

Never reveal all aspects of your personality nor all of your opinions, beliefs, or intentions at once. Be selective in what you reveal and what you withhold. Resist the urge to always display the same demeanor and behavior all the time. Embrace flexibility, allowing yourself to adapt and change as situations evolve. Be authentic, but a bit mysterious.

This keeps others intrigued and wanting to know more about you, prevents others from exploiting your vulnerabilities, and enables you to shift your demeanor and/or your perspective to adapt to the situation. Giving yourself time to reveal and others time to discover the multifaceted person you are builds understanding, trust, and respect while safeguarding your individuality and integrity. It also keeps them guessing.

August 20

Amor Fati

Acceptance of oneself and the world is the portal to understanding how to improve ourselves and the world.

Unlike other Earthly species, which accept life just as it is, humans often question the meaning of life, the why of our existence and the world around us. Yet, there are no easy answers to those questions, some of which are unanswerable. Instead of searching for the meaning of life, we should focus on accepting and living life.

Acceptance doesn't mean satisfaction. Some aspects of human life will and should disgust us—injustice, hypocrisy, inhumanity, poverty, greed, violence, to name a few. Instead of questioning why something bad is happening to us or in the world, we should be asking what we can do to improve ourselves and the world. This is only possible if we first acknowledge that the wrongdoing exists.

See things as they are. Strive to improve yourself and the world around you. You are free to choose, but recognize that every choice changes your future. There is nothing wrong with being wrong, unless you refuse to change when presented with new credible, valid information.

August 21

Mortality

Why do we fear death, but live as if we are immortal?

As mortals, we experience an inherent fear of knowing our time on this earth is limited. Yet, we simultaneously live our lives as if we have endless time as we defer pursuing our desires, ambitions, and aspirations. Maybe it is because our consciousness cannot fully grasp the concept of no longer living, of not having sufficient time to achieve them. Or maybe our aspirations are so profoundly ingrained or so grandiose that we fear them just like we fear death. We tend to look forward and believe we have adequate time to plan to start but we don't consider the time to finish. As is, some of us act as though we believe we are really immortal and have unlimited time. But we don't. Although our mortal duration is unknown, it is limited and can end unexpectedly.

Don't let the shadow of death nor the delusion of unfathomable time obscure your life. Strive to be the best you can be, for inner peace and fulfillment. Live as a mortal, fully and in the moment, aware but not frightened of your mortality or your wildest dreams.

August 22

Emotion

The sense of doubt and self-worthlessness can be inflicted by external sources but exists deep inside you.

In a world full of critics, remember that their opinions stem from limited perceptions, not absolute truth, and they may be a means of manipulation. While criticism naturally triggers emotional responses—such as anger, defensiveness, and self-doubt—don't let these reactions diminish your self-worth. Instead of internalizing others' judgments, focus on your genuine capabilities. Acknowledge both your strengths and limitations. Build your self-image around your achievements, character, and intentions rather than on external validation.

When criticism strikes, resist the urge to prove critics wrong or to spiral into self-doubt. Be your own advocate. Recognize your inherent value beyond others' opinions. Many seek to undermine your confidence for their own advantage; don't become your own worst critic. The path to resilience lies in accepting yourself fully. During difficult moments, remind yourself of your accomplishments and unique qualities. Choose self-compassion over self-criticism. Remember: you alone hold the authority to define your worth. You can be your best friend or worst enemy; it is your choice.

August 23

Awareness

Self and situational awareness are the cornerstones of both progress and effective change.

It is interesting to watch people standing in queues. When their line doesn't seem or actually move quickly enough, you see their impatience. When their line moves faster than others, you see their relief. When someone jumps from a slow-moving to a fast-moving line only to have the queue come to a halt, you see their frustration. This paradox applies to far more important life decisions, too. Too often, our emotions get the better of us, so we jump to another line only to discover we're on the wrong track or facing a dead-end.

Beware of the urge to jump into or move toward something that seems better. Look beyond your initial impression to get a clear vision of what's actually there. Reaffirm why you chose the path you're on, and survey how far you've come and where you're headed. Determine whether the path you're on is still the right one for you. If not or if you're just itching for change, stay the course while you explore other options and until there is proof of a better path for you. Make change your informed choice, not hasty decision based on anyone else's choice or suggestion or your impatience.

August 24

Social Thought

By holding onto the past too tightly, we hold ourselves back from our future.

The past is behind us. It cannot be changed. But when the past is our main or only focus, whether through memories or mementos, it can become an encumbrance. Dwelling on the past to the exclusion of the present or future will warp what did or will happen. Repeatedly telling stories of our past can be annoying and seem self-absorbed to the people in our lives. Listening to and communicating with others, rather than performing skits from our past, is far more rewarding for everyone.

Those who cling to their past usually do so because they don't embrace today or perceive a future. They think their past is all they have, even though every day presents opportunities to live. Ironically, their death grip on the past can put a stranglehold on them and their future.

Don't allow your reverence of your past rob you of your potential to relish your now and your future.

August 25

Action

Facing fear with bold action guides success and averts failure.

Face Every Adversity Ruthlessly (FEAR), as fear is nothing more than an emotion to be acknowledged and used to your advantage. Fear motivates in the near term, while desire motivates in the long term. In pursuit of every objective, we will face challenges and situations that are uncomfortable and scary, drawing our deepest fears to the surface. What is the root of our fears? Is it not wanting to experience failure, embarrassment, loss, change, injury, or maybe even success? All of those are possible, whether we live our life assertively or passively.

Prepare as best you can for the known as well as the unknown. Brace yourself for failure as you seek success. Without success, you don't learn how to avoid defeat. Without failure, you don't learn to extend your limits, which can lead to loss of inertia and stagnation. Failure and success are simultaneously symbiotic and opposites. Work with them together, and face your fears ruthlessly.

August 26

Problem Solving

Knowledge in the absence of common-sense limits understanding.

Common sense is one of the most underrated human characteristics. It is the ability to see commonplace things as they are, to dismiss things that are nonsensical or deceitful, and to act accordingly. Many intellectual, religious, and worldly people struggle to see simple things in life. Although they may have extensive knowledge and experiences, they have limited wisdom—the ability to put what they've learned to use. They may also confine the breadth of their knowledge and experiences to their areas of interest and expertise.

Common sense is a form of wisdom that is acquired through wisely applying what you have learned through observation, experience, contemplation, and your own moral compass. Explore everything that interests you or poses unanswered questions. Embrace the basic realities of life, good and bad. Apply what you learn wisely, guided by your common sense. Your knowledge and experiences will be well-spent, benefitting all, and your wisdom will grow.

August 27

Resilience

Opportunity is always knocking. It is the wise who hear it.

Opportunity doesn't knock randomly or selectively. It is ever-present, but we're often too distracted by the chaos around us to notice. Those who lean into chaos to look for opportunities are the ones who recognize and pursue opportunity. Many things can cause you to miss the chances life offers; don't let timidity or inattention be among them. To the keen observer, chaos is not always chaotic. The world is full of possibilities, but they are only accessible to those who are observant and prepared to act.

Recognize and be ready to take chances whenever and however they are presented. Sharpen your senses, hone your skills, and keep a proactive attitude. Success is not a matter of luck but of readiness and responsiveness. Your ability to discern the opportunities, however vague, will set you apart. The knock of opportunity is constant; it's up to you to answer it.

August 28

Amor Fati

Life has times of turbulence and of tranquility. Each is valuable and should be enjoyed.

During your lifetime, you will experience times of tremendous upheaval and of steady calm. While periods of turmoil might feel overwhelming, that is when you are living at your edge—an edge that might strengthen you or be detrimental to you. Periods of stability might allow more time for reflection and recovery; they can also lead to boredom and loss of focus. During calmer times in your life, relish what you have done and prepare for the next episode of churning exhilaration.

This ebb and flow life is beneficial and gives you the opportunity to find balance. For muscles to build strength and stamina, they are purposely exposed to periods of increasing stress, followed by a predetermined time for recovery. Utilize the concept of periodized training as you move through life. Recognize that neither tranquility nor turbulence will last forever, and make the most of both, as each is needed to make you stronger physically, mentally and spiritually.

August 29

Mortality

Embracing life illuminates the richness of life and leaves a life well-lived in the shadow of death.

Given the transient nature of our existence, most people become more aware of mortality at some point—and in response, some begin to shrink from life. Embrace the present with open arms, cherish your relationships deeply, and pursue your passions with unwavering dedication and intention. Focus on what truly matters, and learn to let go of things that don't or are beyond your influence. Reflect on the impermanence of life, and let it inspire you to live more fully, love more profoundly, and act with greater compassion. Understand that every breath you take is a precious gift, a reminder to stay grounded and centered amidst the chaos. Free yourself from unnecessary stress and anxiety; allow space for joy, creativity, and meaningful connections.

Live with a sense of purpose and urgency—being fully present, making conscious choices, and savoring the richness of each experience. That doesn't mean rushing through life at a frantic pace. It means prioritizing how you spend your time, living with intention and a deep sense of gratitude for the life you're living and the gift of time.

August 30

Emotion

Ego is a person's subconscious assessment of their value. Self-delusion can be disabling and destructive to oneself and others.

Ego is the voice deep within that continually whispers to us how we perceive our contributions, esteem, and worth—especially in contrast to others. A healthy ego gives us the self-awareness, confidence, and impetus to face adversity, pursue opportunities, and improve ourselves. An unhealthy ego exaggerates or fabricates evidence of our superiority or inferiority. Such distortions or delusions of grandeur or insignificance can drive someone's thoughts and emotions toward actions that may be detrimental to themselves or others.

Just as you can feel and hear the wind and see how trees bend and yield to its force, so too can you sense your ego. Unlike the wind, your ego is a force of your human nature that you can control. Use your mind and spirit to recognize when your self-perception is off-kilter and you need to adjust your inner lens. Be honest with and kind to yourself, neither overvaluing or undervaluing yourself. Keep your ego in check, and it will serve you well.

August 31

Awareness

True leadership comes from within and reveals the path forward.

Leaders who, like puppeteers, play with the fears and adversities of others seek only to manipulate insecurities and struggles for their own gain. Their tactics often involve creating false hope and a sense of dependency, making you believe their deceitful claim that only they can provide the answers to your problems.

Beware of such charlatans, and follow your own lead. Recognize your own worth, and appreciate what you have, rather than focusing on what you lack and others might have. Never lose sight of who you are and what matters to you. Seek to understand all facets of an issue, problem, or condition. Find mentors and leaders whose integrity and actions inspire you to be your best self and to think independently. Surround yourself with people who uplift and support you.

When you are true to yourself and run the claims of so-called "leaders" through your filters, no one can lead you astray. Your decisions and actions will come from your awareness of yourself and others. Then, not only will you find peace, but you will also become a beacon of hope and inspiration for others.

September

September 1

Social Thought

A free mind pursues knowledge with excitement and scrutiny. A captured mind unquestionably absorbs whatever input, fact or fiction, it is given.

The quest for knowledge is fraught with moments of doubt and exhilaration. As free-thinkers navigate the complex landscape of ideas and experiences, they are willing to both consider and question everything in their path. In their fervent pursuit of knowledge, they are unafraid to confront uncomfortable truths or to dismantle long-held beliefs. The free mind is a beacon of intellectual freedom, constantly pushing the boundaries of what is known and what is possible.

A captured mind is a passive recipient of what others think and believe, including misinformation. Those with captured minds accept falsehoods and distortions without resistance. They do not question or doubt the "knowledge" they've adopted, nor do they seek information and experiences beyond their rigid frame of reference. The captured mind is chained by dogma, restricted by propaganda, and stifled by conformity. It is a tragic symbol of intellectual subjugation. Incapable of critical thought and innovation, it is lost in a sea of mediocrity and misinformation.

Free your mind by exploring and evaluating new ideas, beliefs, and experiences. Learn from both trusted and unfamiliar sources. Be discerning about who and what you rely on for information. Strive to be open-minded, and a world of knowledge will open to you.

September 2

Awareness

The purpose of a tradition is diminished or lost when the tradition becomes an expectation or obligation.

Traditions and customs have been a part of human culture for centuries, and today most of us practice numerous personal, social, cultural, and spiritual traditions and customs. Sometimes, these events are meaningful to us, especially if we have created or adapted them to suit us. Many of us, however, find ourselves following and propagating traditions and customs that we don't understand, value, and/or enjoy. When that happens, those practices intended to honor and celebrate life instead become duties we fulfill with little or no joy or meaning.

Participating in and supporting such insignificant expectations and obligations diverts your energy, time, and focus from things you want and need to do to sustain and enhance your life. If adherence to a tradition or custom has become a duty or encumbrance, perhaps it's time to start fresh with a practice that brings value to you and those around you. Or you can just let it go and use that time as you choose.

September 3
Problem Solving
Scapegoating has no positive, problem solving agenda. Its sole purpose is to propagate hate, fear, and dysfunction.

Those who habitually find someone or something to blame for their failures are humanity's cowards. They don't really want or attempt to solve problems or to confront the systemic issues facing their greater community. They want power and authority without responsibility or accountability. They find it easier to disparage others rather than work with others to alleviate discord and create solutions. The greater their power, the greater their potential to fail and to harm. Hold such irresponsible cowards accountable for their failures, scapegoating being among the biggest.

September 4

Resilience

Being dependent can be devastatingly demoralizing.

Each of us has been dependent upon someone or something in our past and will be again in our future. It is beneficial for children and teens to be somewhat but decreasingly dependent upon their parents. Many of us will be increasingly dependent on others in our elder years. Otherwise, dependency—upon an organization, person, or drug—is debilitating. It drains us of our self-will, self-worth, and independence. It makes us feel vulnerable and out of control.

Identify any dependencies you might have—whether physical, emotional, mental, financial, familial, social, or institutional. Name them. Examine them, and determine why you feel or became dependent. Resist mental and emotional dependency. Resist the death spiral of substance dependence, including pharmaceuticals. Even if you are dependent on drugs or alcohol or dependent on other people financially or socially, you can still control your thoughts, emotions, reactions, and actions. You can choose and work toward independence from any substance, person, organization, or situation. Trust yourself. Find the self-determination and whatever professional support you need to free yourself from dependency and claim your independence.

September 5

Amor Fati
You find what you focus on, good or bad.

When you concentrate your thoughts and energy on something, it tends to become more prominent in your life. This means that if you focus on positive things, you'll notice more positivity around you. Conversely, if you dwell on the negative, you may find that negativity seems to grow. If you look for joy, you will find it even through the suffering. If you look for pain, you will surely find it too. Be mindful of where you direct your attention and efforts, as it can significantly influence your overall outlook and experiences.

September 6

Mortality

Your destiny cannot be found in any mystical or religious manuscript; you must create it.

Your destiny is not predetermined, nor is it a singular outcome within the absolute control of anything or anyone. It is your life's path, for you and you alone to determine and follow. Although you may find inspiration in religious and spiritual teachings and practices, they can't and shouldn't dictate your decisions or actions, which are the true determinants of your achievements and your future.

Neither is there an ethereal force guiding you to your fate. There is only you, making choices every moment of every day. It is those choices and the things you do (or don't do) that open and close the doors of opportunity, that send you in the wrong direction or lead you to a dead end, that empower your achievements or enable your failures. You are the driving force of every day of your life and your future, right up until your physical body finally fails. Trusting in yourself is far more important and effective than trusting in any of humanity's created faiths.

September 7

Emotion

Humility is as underrated as confidence is overrated.

Humility, an often overlooked and underappreciated character trait, holds as much importance to personal growth and societal harmony as does confidence, which is often overemphasized and excessively lauded. While confidence can propel us forward, an excess of it can lead to arrogance of our strengths and blind spots to our weaknesses. Humility, on the other hand, fosters openness to learning, empathy, and continuous self-improvement. These are essential qualities for navigating the complexities of life and relationships. Be confident in your humility.

September 8

Awareness

Can you see yourself in everyone you meet? You are there and they are within you. Look closely and make your actions such that you like what you see.

Each of us is intricately connected to every individual we encounter, and they, in turn, become an integral part of our being. This interconnectedness manifests through a subtle exchange of energy, ideas, and emotions. Our actions, words, and thoughts gradually permeate the consciousness of those around us, just as theirs seep into our individual psyches. This process of mutual influence occurs both overtly and covertly, sometimes in ways we may not immediately perceive.

Given this, it becomes imperative to exercise great care in your actions, your words, and even your thoughts. Strive to ensure that what you project into the world aligns with your highest values and aspirations. This will cultivate an environment in which positivity, compassion, and wisdom can flourish. Remember, the energy you emit will inevitably be reflected back to you, shaping your immediate experiences and the collective consciousness of which you are a part.

September 9

Social Thought

Evil preys on the self-consumed. Its deceit is seductive and alluring. It promises what you want in exchange for your blind loyalty and the surrender of your self-will.

You know them. You've seen them. The ones who are so self-consumed they cannot see how self-destructive they have become. Their need for self-gratification is so powerful it leads them down a path in which they are devoid of willpower and are loyal only to themselves, to their own detriment. Their self-absorption becomes a silent, evil parasite that dominates and slowly consumes their spirit—controlling all their actions with a self-centered focus at the exclusion of all else.

September 10

Action

To master anything, you must trust and remain faithful to the process.

There are no shortcuts to becoming a master of anything. Mastery comes from arduous hours of repetition, intense focus on the fundamentals at every step, and an unyielding faith and belief in the process. It is often achieved with rapid advancements mixed with routine setbacks. If you are not experiencing setbacks, you are not pressing your limits and you will not master even the fundamentals. You will learn the most from these setbacks. Embrace them, and analyze them. Bring your knowledge, best efforts, and determination to every task, every time. Don't give up your dreams. Chase them, and never fear them.

September 11

Problem Solving

There is power in selective silence, sincere questioning, and calming words.

We live in a cacophonous world filled with distractions and with people incessantly voicing their opinions or parroting those of others. Silence, however, makes many uncomfortable. Yet, it holds immense power. When you listen silently, people often feel compelled to fill the void, usually revealing more than they intended. There is strength in silence.

Ask questions with genuine interest, then pause to allow the other person(s) to answer, and listen closely. Respond to questions, challenges, and interruptions with measured words and in a steady voice. Matching the agitated tones and behaviors of others only exacerbates the chaos and diminishes your position. Staying calm and using controlled speech and strategic silence can bolster your stance, even when others lose their composure.

September 12

Resilience

You have the power inside you to seek the truth.

Within you lies an innate ability to pursue, uncover, and recognize truth. This internal power, which stems from intellectual curiosity and critical thinking, drives your quest for knowledge and understanding. It empowers you to question, investigate, and discern, guiding you through the complex landscape of information and misinformation. By harnessing this inherent strength, you can navigate the path to enlightenment, continually expanding your understanding of the world and yourself.

September 13

Amor Fati

Change is constantly happening to and around you.

Some people fear change. Some claim change is hard. Yet, nature is in a constant flux of change, to which we must adapt. The world of human creation also changes continually, and we must adapt to that as well. So, too, must we adapt to the changes within ourselves and our personal lives. The first critical steps to managing change are to know yourself and to accept the inevitability of change.

Know and accept who you are and how you wish to change. Love what you are now as much as you love who you are changing into. Embrace change, facing it willingly, purposefully, and fearlessly. The better able you are to anticipate, welcome, and adapt to change, the more attuned you will be to the nature of all things and the world around you.

September 14

Mortality

The dormancy of winter is not about death or hiding from life. It's about survival and the promise of tomorrow.

Everyone goes through periods of decreased activity over the course of their lives. As we age and/or our health declines, most of us curtail our pursuits and reduce our pace. Being in a temporary lull or an extended deceleration does not mean it's time to rest on our laurels or quit life. We can rest and rejuvenate, plan, and prepare while we continue to be as active as we're able and choose to be. It is possible to recuperate and still be vital. And sometimes, the best way to build or sustain strength is to take a break or slow down.

Embrace the cyclical nature of life. Although periods of apparent dormancy, like winter, may appear to resemble death, they are merely remedies to depletion and precursors to flourishing. Draw upon the wellspring of strength that exists deep within your core. Tap into the wisdom and resilience accumulated throughout your past experiences. Each day, consciously prepare yourself for personal growth and renewal, even in the winter of your life.

September 15

Emotion

Anger breeds hate. Love breeds peace. Acceptance dissipates hate and brings at least peace of mind.

The propagation of hatred inevitably fosters more anger and hatred, while the cultivation of peace fosters acceptance and tranquility. These two states cannot co-exist, nor can one directly transform into the other. Hate cannot spontaneously evolve into peace, nor can love suddenly devolve into anger. To achieve a state of peace, whether in the world around us or within ourselves, the presence of anger must be dispelled. This process begins with acceptance—a neutral state that serves as a steppingstone away from negativity and toward positivity.

Only by consciously replacing hatred with acceptance can we hope to create the conditions necessary for peace to flourish. The journey from hatred to peace through acceptance is essential for societal harmony as well as for individual peace of mind and emotional well-being.

September 16

Awareness

The best antidotes to external stressors are self-awareness and self-care.

We are all too easily distracted by the chaotic world around us. The deadlines, the pressure, the need to keep up appearances and personas all become barriers to our own success. Personal success is really about finding oneself within this chaotic morass. When we get too caught up in these external distractions, we find it difficult to focus inward and often lose sight of our spirituality and sense of self.

If you find yourself distracted by the chaos in your life or the world around you, shift your focus to what you control—your thoughts, beliefs, emotions, goals, and actions. Concentrating on your own body, mind, spirit, and well-being isn't being ego-centric; it is spiritual survival. You control only yourself; let the rest just rest.

September 17

Social Thought

Don't make a show of your religion or possessions. Rather, quietly enjoy and selflessly share them.

Many amongst us feel compelled to overtly flaunt their faith and wealth, making both seem like sideshows. Refrain from ostentatious displays of religious devotion and/or material wealth. Instead, cultivate a quiet and humble appreciation for your spiritual beliefs and possessions. Find private joy in their personal significance. Moreover, embrace the spirit of generosity by sharing these blessings with others in a humble and selfless manner. If asked, share without seeking agreement, consensus, recognition, praise, or reciprocation. This fosters contentment and promotes a sense of community. It allows both you and others to benefit from the true value of your faith and resources.

September 18

Action

Snap judgments lead to rash reactions. Informed judgments lead to rational deductions.

Now more than ever, with today's information glut, our reaction to incoming information is based on its source, with a tendency to view certain sources more favorably than others. Our experiences shape how we evaluate the legitimacy, accuracy, relevance, and value of information sources. However, those same experiences can bias us, which can subconsciously lead to discriminatory judgments and potentially poor reactions.

Instead of reacting immediately to something you've read or heard or seen, it is wise to not only consider but also to assess the source, regardless of its familiarity or unfamiliarity to you. Misunderstood intentions can result in unfortunate responses. Before you react, take a little time to scrutinize both the source and the content.

September 19

Problem Solving

An open, agile mind sees both hidden opportunities and opportunity in adversity.

Just as opportunity is always knocking, so is its antithesis, adversity, always lurking in the shadows, ready to present itself and potentially block our way. Among the adversities presenting the greatest barriers to success are our inability to recognize and pursue opportunity and our inability to recognize and overcome potential threats. Failing to recognize and/or to act upon both the positive and negative possibilities before us results in missed chances, regret, and stagnation. This lack of awareness and this hesitation or resistance to action does not serve a proactive quest for growth and success.

Acknowledging the ever-present nature of both potentially beneficial and potentially detrimental circumstances can enable you to recognize both opportunity and adversity. Cultivating a heightened awareness of these two opposing forces will empower you to seize favorable moments and navigate challenges with greater resilience and wisdom.

September 20

Resilience

The most rewarding journeys often involve traversing the most demanding terrains and overcoming personal trials.

The path of righteousness often diverges from the route of least resistance, presenting challenges and obstacles along the way. It is precisely this arduous journey that holds the greatest potential for personal growth, societal progress, and lasting fulfillment. Embracing this path requires sacrifice and perseverance. However, it ultimately leads to a life of integrity, purpose, and profound satisfaction.

Summon the inner strength and moral fortitude to pursue goals and actions that are ethically sound, beneficial to society, and meaningful to you.

September 21

Amor Fati

When we embrace and engage in, rather than merely endure, each stage of life, we live more fully, joyfully, and gratefully.

Life is a river, beginning with a trickling, unassuming start at its headwaters. It flows through the sometimes-turbulent periods of adolescence, navigates the swift currents and protective eddies of adulthood, and meanders through the tranquil doldrums of senior years. Finally, your weary essence returns to the vast ocean, completing the cycle. Accept the cycle and the stage of life you are in, not looking back too harshly or looking forward too eagerly.

September 22

Mortality

Viewing your past with a dispassionate eye, neither overly positive nor negative, will give you a better perspective of today and tomorrow.

Many of us, across the spectrum of ages, spend time reminiscing about our past. Recalling memories can be either a positive or negative exercise, depending on how you view and how much you think about past experiences.

When looking back on your life, resist the temptation to view it with excessive optimism or pessimism. Recall and appreciate your past, but don't dwell on it. Savor the good memories, but don't romanticize them. Examine difficult memories, but don't wallow in them. Letting things go frees you from the shackles of overly powerful thoughts and emotions associated with both negative and positive experiences.

This clear-eyed reflection of your past serves as a valuable tool for gaining insight into your present circumstances and shaping your future trajectory. It enables you to identify patterns, learn from successes and failures, and make more informed choices. It empowers you to navigate your life journey with enhanced clarity and purpose. Never read your own press; you might start to believe it.

September 23

Emotion

The more you know and understand, the less you fear the unknown—even though the more you know, the more you realize there is more to learn.

The acquisition of knowledge and understanding serves as a powerful antidote to the fear of the unknown. Expand your intellectual horizons and deepen your comprehension of the world around you. You'll find that the shadows of uncertainty will begin to recede. This doesn't only illuminate the known; paradoxically, it also sheds light on the vastness of what is still undiscovered. Becoming more aware of the immense expanse of the unknown lying beyond your current grasp doesn't intensify fear; instead, it fosters a sense of curiosity and wonder.

The more you learn, the more comfortable you become with the concept of the unknown and with expanding your knowledge. You become keenly aware that the unknown is not a threat, but rather an opportunity for further exploration and growth. This shift in perspective allows you to approach life's uncertainties with greater confidence and less trepidation. It does so even as you humbly acknowledge the limitless nature of what's yet to be understood.

September 24

Awareness

All things are linked through relativity and perspective.

Every event may seem unique to us, but it is also perceived uniquely by those experiencing it at the same time. Each of us, with our own special viewpoint and personal history, interprets the same situation differently. Because of this, we cannot know the whole truth based solely on our perspective, which is not only unique to us in that moment but also influenced by our personal biases. The interlinking of observations and perspectives forms a kaleidoscopic mosaic of the real, full truth. Always seek different perspectives. Don't fear them; consider, embrace, and incorporate them.

September 25

Social Thought

You should have a clear, realistic view of deception, not a misconception of reality.

We daily confront disinformation in many forms as political and social factions try to sway our opinions and gain our support. A clear antidote to the misinformation spin is to cultivate a clear understanding of reality. This enables us to distinguish between misleading projections and genuine insights, which fosters a more grounded worldview. Critical thought and assessment allow us to better navigate the complexities of our experiences juxtaposed with the illusions being propagated.

Don't be afraid to challenge what you see, hear, and read. Analyze everything from as many angles and sources as you can to make more informed decisions and to illuminate deceptions and misconceptions.

September 26

Action

There is a direct correlation between perfectionism and procrastination, between procrastination and failure, and between failure and inaction.

The hallmark of those who always seem to be treading water is their perpetual state of no forward motion. They languish in a cycle of endless waiting, constantly seeking the elusive perfect conditions, the ideal moment, or the flawless circumstances. In their misguided pursuit of perfection, they invariably discover some minute flaw or imperfection that serves as a convenient excuse for their continued inertia. This relentless quest for an unattainable state of perfection becomes a self-imposed barrier to progress and achievement.

The wisdom lies not in waiting for the perfect alignment of all factors, but in having the courage to initiate action despite imperfections. Progress and success are born from the willingness to begin—to take that first step, regardless of the perceived shortcomings of the present situation. The key to breaking free from a cycle of inaction is profoundly simple: just start. Embrace the imperfections, acknowledge the challenges, and move forward with determination and purpose.

September 27

Problem Solving

Personal and professional success are cultivated through both inquisitive discovery and intellectual discernment.

Curiosity and skepticism can be friends or foes in the pursuit of wisdom and goals. Curiosity empowers us to seek and discover new information and experiences, while skepticism empowers us to question and evaluate information and experiences. Left unchecked, either can lead to detrimental outcomes. An overly skeptical mindset can foster negativity and erode self-confidence, potentially hindering personal growth and opportunities. Unbridled curiosity, while often lauded as a positive trait, may expose one to unnecessary risks and impulsive decision-making. The key lies in judiciously harnessing these two traits.

Strive to keep an equilibrium between curiosity and skepticism. Allow these traits to complement rather than conflict with each other. By exercising rational thought and keeping emotional composure, you can navigate the fine line between productive curiosity and perceptive skepticism. This balance will enable you to critically evaluate situations while remaining open to new experiences and knowledge, leading to more informed and measured actions.

September 28

Resilience

Self-delusion of one's value, importance, and irreplaceability has been the downfall of many. Don't join their ranks.

There are a lot of amazing people in this world. Yet, not one of them has all the answers, and every one of them is replaceable. Professionally, you likely assumed the role you have from someone who thought they were irreplaceable. They were mistaken, and so are you. You and your thoughts and beliefs are neither the default nor the end-all. No matter your opinion of your importance or the superiority of your intellect and analysis, leave room for the contrarian and conflicting ideas of others. Challenge your own perspectives, and continually strive to improve yourself.

September 29

Amor Fati

The richness of life is measured by the sum of what is gained from life's ups and downs.

It's easy to be thankful for pleasant things. Being thankful for unpleasant things is more challenging but equally important, because life's struggles give you a greater appreciation for everything. Although it can be hard to find anything positive in an uncomfortable situation, trying times and situations can and should bring out the best in us, not the worst.

Embrace where fate has brought you, recognizing that all your past actions are integral to where you are and what you are facing now. Your karma, attitude, and actions create your future. Be grateful for all aspects of your life—the joys and sorrows, gains and losses, calm and storms. Life is beautiful and amazing, from beginning to end.

September 30

Mortality
Living each day to its fullest is about trying to do your best and enjoying the moment, not about doing outlandish things.

The concept of living each day as if it were your last is often misunderstood. It's not about engaging in reckless or extravagant activities, nor is it about abandoning all responsibilities. Rather, it is a philosophy that encourages mindful living and purposeful action, day by day. This approach to life involves striving to do your utmost in every situation, keeping self-control, and finding joy and appreciation in the present moment. It's about making conscious choices that align with your values and goals. It's treating others with kindness and respect while savoring the simple pleasures that each day brings.

By adopting this mindset, you cultivate a deeper sense of gratitude for life's experiences, both big and small, good and bad. You develop a greater awareness of how you spend your time and energy. You neither succumb to complacency nor take your days for granted. You live each day as if it were your last, embracing life fully with intention and appreciation. You only have so many laps around the sun; make each step you take count.

October

October 1

Emotion

The desire for things truncates your greatest asset: your capacity for reasoned thought and cripples your free will

---

The uncontrolled desire for possessions can overwhelm our thoughts and drive us to unreasonable acts. It can cause us to hoard and to lust for wealth, power, and prestige. Admiration of things lends itself to envying things that belong to others. Sometimes we love our things more than people and more than our own thoughts. Our free will, our freedom of thought, our ability to control our judgment, choices and responses (the Stoicism concept of *prohairsesis*) is crippled by our desire of assets rather than thought.

To exercise our capability to make reasoned, virtuous decisions and choices, we must let go of things, even if they are treasures of our past or mementos of those we've lost. We must detach from our attachments to things and ideas. Doing so frees your mind to examine, question, and remain flexible to both your own ideas and those of others.

October 2

Awareness

Recognizing your potential unleashes and guides your actions.

A solitary grain of sand, when joined with countless other grains of sand being carried along by the relentless flow of a river, can contribute to the carving of majestic canyons. So too can a single individual, through persistent effort and collaboration, bring about monumental change. This natural phenomenon serves as a powerful metaphor for the potential that lies within every person and the potential of collective human achievement. It reminds us that seemingly small actions, when sustained over time and combined with the efforts of others, can reshape the landscape of our world.

Approach your endeavors with energetic persistence, unwavering dedication, and a willingness to work alongside others. This can open the door to accomplishing truly mighty things, which will leave an indelible mark on the world.

October 3

Social Thought

A free, civilized society doesn't ban people, books, or ideas.

Enlightened societies are built and survive on the basic tenets of unrestricted access to all forms of information, ideas, and creative expression. History has shown the horror of isolated and controlled thought, suppression of human expression, and oppression of select groups of people. Such precepts and practices result in collapsed societies and the eradication of civil liberties. As you walk the trail of knowledge, you will encounter a bifurcation, with one path leading to the parched land of Ignorance Is Bliss and the other leading to the lush land of Knowledge Is Power. The choice is yours; choose wisely.

October 4

Action

The goal of being the best human you can be is a big enough goal.

Throughout our lives, we think about and set for ourselves a lot of admirable goals. But maybe the most important goal is the simplest one: for each of us to be the best human being, the best person, we can be. Nothing more, because there really isn't anything more. Nothing less, because anything less falls short of our highest potential—not in what we achieve, but in who we can become

Cultivating these essential qualities will help you (and each of us) achieve this goal:

- A steadfast certainty in your judgment, allowing you to make decisions with confidence and clarity
- A commitment to taking action that benefits the greater good, ensuring that your choices positively affect not only yourself but also those around you
- A deep-seated sense of gratitude for each and every experience that comes your way, regardless of its nature

This approach to life promotes mindfulness, ethical behavior, and a positive outlook, all of which contribute to your personal growth and societal well-being while also helping you achieve the ultimate goal.

October 5

Problem Solving

You aren't in life's struggle alone and neither should anyone else be.

Your life and the bounty you've obtained are not solely of your making. You've had help along the way. Some help was obvious, some anonymous, some intentional, and some inadvertent, but help nonetheless. This aid helped you solve problems, gave you opportunities, and provided the support you needed during good times and bad. You now might be in the position to lend aid, and all should be invited to your life's table.

Thank those who've been an invaluable source of support, or unexpectedly and graciously filled a gap, or sacrificed on your behalf long ago and may now be or feel essentially forgotten. Acknowledge the riches you've received and make a conscious effort to reciprocate them. Touch the present and reach for the future while never forgetting the people in your past who deserve your recognition and those who need your help.

October 6

Resilience

Completion earns rest; rest allows renewal. Renewal encourages new goals; new goals advance new efforts.

After completing an objective or a phase in life, we benefit from taking a respite, allowing ourselves time for renewal and reflection. This rest period allows us to recharge and prepare for new beginnings. When starting the next objective, approach it with purpose. Begin by defining your goals. Without clear goals, new beginnings can become aimless. Setting defined goals provides direction and gives structure to your aspirations, effectively channeling your energy and resources. Set meaningful goals to infuse each life chapter with intention. This will add depth to your journey and maximize your growth potential.

October 7

Amor Fati

There is no inherent meaning or predisposition of natural occurrences, good or bad.

The universe is in a constant state of flux. Randomness and chaos play integral roles in shaping the course of events. This perpetual motion is not governed by any divine orchestration or supreme cosmic puppeteer pulling the strings behind the scenes. Instead, it is a vast, intricate tapestry of interconnected occurrences, each unfolding without preordained meaning or predetermined purpose. In this grand perspective, events happen—neither intrinsically good nor bad but neutral in their essence. Natural occurrences are not punishments or rewards; they just are.

It is our own views and interpretations of these events that imbue them with significance. The power lies not in the events themselves but in our reaction to them. How we choose to respond to the myriad happenings in our lives becomes the true determinant of our subsequent actions and experiences. This understanding empowers us to approach life's twists and turns with equanimity. Our perspective and reaction hold the key to navigating life's unpredictable currents.

October 8

Mortality

Life is a creation that expires when we die. Our legacy lives on, for better or worse.

Your existence in this world is a remarkable creation unfolding throughout your years. It is a unique mosaic of your experiences, choices, and interactions. This personal narrative reaches its conclusion when you draw your final breath, marking the end of your physical journey. Yet, the impact of your life extends far beyond your mortal span.

Your legacy, the sum total of your actions, ideas, and influences on others, continues to resonate long after you're gone. This enduring imprint on the world can manifest in myriad ways—through the memories you leave behind, the lives you've touched, the work you've accomplished, and/or the values you've instilled in others. Whether this legacy is viewed positively or negatively depends on the nature of your actions and their lasting effects. While life itself is finite, its echoes can be eternal. This serves as a powerful reminder of everyone's potential to shape the world, even beyond their own lifetime.

October 9

Emotion
Resistance to change reflects deep-seated fear.

Reluctance to change is a natural human response to the unknown, and it is often deeply rooted in fear and uncertainty. Change can disrupt our comfort zones and challenge our established routines. Successful change management hinges on our ability to understand and address the underlying fears of change.

Evaluate your personal reluctance to any change. Your reaction might be different if the change is anticipated or sudden. Yet, it remains a change you may be forced to face. Do so with a clear vision of your goals, and align the change as best you can for your benefit.

When others are affected by change, help them find personal benefits within the change. Listen to their concerns, then explain and demonstrate how the change can align with their individual goals and values, giving them a sense of self control.

This personalized, proactive approach to change can transform resistance into acceptance and even enthusiasm. It empowers us and/or the person(s) we're helping to be active participants in the process of change, rather than passive recipients of imposed alterations.

October 10

Awareness

The interplay of timing, positioning, and awareness empowers our ability to capitalize on opportunities and forms the cornerstone of success.

Success often hinges on the delicate balance of being in the right place at the right time while being in a state of readiness to act decisively. This readiness means being mentally and physically prepared to recognize and take appropriate action to pursue potential opportunity when it presents itself.

In our ever-changing world, opportunities emerge constantly and are often available fleetingly. The ability to quickly recognize opportunity, discern whether it is right for you, and respond effectively is essential. This requires a heightened state of awareness and preparedness that allows you to perceive subtle cues and patterns that others might overlook and to position yourself advantageously. Stay alert for opportunities, and be ready to seize every opportunity that might advance your journey.

October 11

Social Thought

The right to freedom of expression and free will are critical human rights for which we should be grateful and vigilantly protective.

In a free society, we often take many things for granted—chief among those are our legal rights to express independent thought and to exercise free will. The ability to read, study, and write what we want without fear of retribution is an extraordinary freedom. It provides us with opportunities for individual growth and expression. A free society also encourages the expression of free will—the personal power to make our own decisions without oppressive authoritarian oversight and control. No one knows you better than you.

Losing our right to either free expression, free will, or both would be catastrophic for us as individuals and as a civilization. Their loss would be devastating, affecting every aspect of our lives and those of future generations. These two freedoms, of expression and free will, are the foundations of human liberty. They are principles worth defending and protecting at all costs. We must never stand by silently if they are challenged—never.

October 12

Action

On one bank of the River Challenge lies Status Quo; on the other bank lies Opportunity. Many people stride incessantly along the bank of Status Quo; few attempt to row their way to Opportunity.

This metaphorical river symbolizes the challenges between us and our goals. While success demands courage to navigate the unknowns and challenges along our path, many people prefer the familiarity and relative stability of the status quo. Too many linger on the bank of complacency to avoid facing obstacles. Some of them make excuses for or blame others for their lack of progress. Whatever their rationale for not crossing the River Challenge, that choice reinforces their perceived limitations and strands them on the bank of Status Quo.

True growth comes from recognizing that opportunities often require stepping out of our comfort zones and taking calculated risks. Exercising resilience to cross the River Challenge to the bank of Opportunity, we unlock possibilities unavailable to those who refuse to make that journey.

October 13

Problem Solving

Strategy in concert with adaptability facilitates progression and success.

Strategy isn't a rigid set of steps or a fixed blueprint. It's a living, flexible plan that evolves to help you achieve your goals. Strategy constantly adapts to changing circumstances and environments while keeping the end goal in sight. To create an effective strategy, you must know your starting point and intended destination, and you must have an idea of what you want to accomplish along the way.

Evaluate various paths to reach your goal. Then, craft an adaptable strategic plan—with specific but not confining or overly defined steps. Periodically reassess your goals and steps, and revise or replace them, if and as needed, to ensure continuous movement toward your intended destination. Think of it as a flowing stream of options leading to ultimate success.

October 14

Resilience

Although only you can control your thoughts, words, actions, and reactions, they can significantly impact others.

You have control over a limited yet powerful domain: your thoughts, words, actions, and reactions. These elements form the core of your personal sphere of influence. It's crucial to recognize that while these aspects are under your command, they have far-reaching implications. Your thoughts shape your perspective. Your words can inspire or discourage. Your actions can create ripples of change. Your reactions can define and affect relationships and situations.

Be acutely aware of the impact the elements you control have on others. Recognize who is impacted, in both your immediate circle and beyond, and how they are affected. Mindfulness in how you exercise this control not only shapes your own life but also significantly affects the lives of others. This creates a web of positive influence that extends far beyond your immediate awareness.

October 15
Amor Fati
Simplicity yields clarity. Clarity yields self-control.

Avoid complicating your life with the self-deception of being in control of or "owning" anything beyond your mind, choices, and will. That misguided notion serves only to cloud your judgment and create unnecessary stress. Embrace the clarity that comes from simplicity. Accept that your true domain of management is limited to three crucial elements:

- Your mind, which shapes your perceptions, emotions, and attitudes

- Your choices, which decide your path and actions
- Your will, which drives your determination and resilience

The only tangible assets you own are the time allotted to you on and the experiences making up your life journey. Time is a finite resource, constantly ticking away. Your experiences form the rich tapestry of your existence. These are the true currencies of life and are far more valuable than any material possessions or illusory control over external circumstances.

Focus on what you can realistically manage, and appreciate what you truly have. This will free you from the burden of trying to control the uncontrollable. It allows you to live more authentically, make more meaningful choices, and find greater satisfaction in your journey through life.

October 16

Mortality

Enjoy the moments of each stage and the cycle of life, because you never know when each will end.

Life unfolds in stages, with each bringing unique joys, challenges, and growth. Embracing these moments with presence allows us to fully experience their beauty. Introspection helps us recognize the lessons and emotions tied to each phase, fostering gratitude and understanding. As time moves forward, we often overlook the significance of fleeting moments until they've passed. By pausing to reflect and cherish what we have now, we cultivate deeper connections and inner peace. Take time to savor each stage, nurture your experiences, and live with intention—for every chapter holds meaning, and none are promised to last forever.

October 17

Emotion

Fear and hope are future-focused emotions that can be a blessing or a curse.

While seemingly opposite, hope and fear share a common characteristic: they shift our focus from the present to an uncertain future. These forward-looking emotions can alert us to opportunities and threats; they can also motivate us to choose actions that enable us to grow and protect ourselves. On the other hand, excessive or unwarranted hope can lead to fixation on potential outcomes, while excessive or unwarranted fear can paralyze us with anxiety. When unchecked, these forward-looking emotions can create a pervasive state of anticipation or dread that overshadows present opportunities and prevents us from fully engaging in current experiences.

Acknowledge and examine feelings of hope or fear when they arise, but don't let either of these emotions control you. Instead, cultivate mindfulness, and focus on what you can influence now. Embrace life's richness as it unfolds by balancing hope and fear with awareness of and attention to the present.

October 18

Awareness

Personal growth is a continuous journey of exploration, discovery, and adaptation.

The journey of self-improvement has an indistinct starting point and no definitive conclusion. It often begins subtly, triggered by a moment of introspection or a desire for change; sometimes, its exact origin remains elusive. Each milestone reached unveils new horizons for development, thus creating an endless cycle of learning and evolution. This perpetual path toward personal growth challenges us to continually reassess our capabilities, adapt to new circumstances, and push beyond our perceived limitations. The absence of a clear endpoint serves as a reminder that true self-improvement is not a destination. It is a continuous process of refinement and discovery that spans the entirety of our lives.

Self-improvement is a journey, taken at your own pace. Enjoy the benefits of self-growth and keep looking for the subtle and obvious calls for betterment and growth. You will forever benefit from the effort.

October 19

Social Thought

History based solely or primarily on the experiences and perspectives of select groups is an incomplete and distorted representation of the past.

Historical narratives have traditionally been written and controlled by the dominant and flourishing groups of a society, not the minorities, downtrodden, or vanquished. This selective recording of experiences and viewpoints, omitting those of marginalized communities and defeated parties, skews perspectives of the past and its influence on the present. As power dynamics evolve, previously silenced voices appear, bringing untold stories and alternative viewpoints to light. Including diverse perspectives in the historical record offers a more complete and nuanced view of past events and their societal impacts. This enables us to move forward with a clearer view of our past, present, and future.

October 20

Action
Calm Thoughts > Calm Words > Calm Deeds

No matter what is going on inside or around you, stay calm. You may feel frantic inside, but exude a calm demeanor. Subdue rash thoughts, harsh words, and reactive actions. Just hold the calm. Your calmness will rule the moment; your chaos will destroy it. Take a breath and a moment to collect your thoughts and calm your emotions. Assess the situation, formulate a plan, and demonstrate your control through calm words and behavior. Your calmness will be infectious and respected.

October 21

Problem Solving

Passion fueled by persistence and tempered with patience facilitates success.

Cultivate a balance between impatience and patience—a dynamic state of *impatient patience*. This mindset involves keeping a burning desire and passionate drive for progress while simultaneously exercising calm discipline in the process of learning and preparation. Embrace the fire of ambition that propels you forward, but temper it with the serene composure required for thorough preparation and thoughtful action. Harness your enthusiasm and urgency without sacrificing the measured steps necessary for sustainable success. Mastering this delicate equilibrium allows you to channel your energy effectively. You will push boundaries while avoiding rash decisions. This will yield more robust and lasting achievements.

October 22

Resilience

Obstacles present unique opportunities to learn, grow, and advance.

Those who have never experienced misfortune are truly the unfortunate. Obstacles are invaluable learning opportunities. They surpass the benefits of easily achieved goals. The challenges they pose and the inherent risk of failure make them particularly significant in personal growth and skill development. When we face obstacles, we are forced to stretch our capabilities, think creatively, and persevere in adversity. While often difficult and sometimes discouraging, these experiences provide a richness of learning that cannot be gained through simple, unchallenging tasks. The process of overcoming obstacles builds resilience. It enhances problem-solving abilities and fosters a growth mindset. Embrace challenges; don't avoid them.

October 23

Amor Fati

Although nature is the physical source of life, nature cannot intentionally affect life.

Humans persistently look for meaning in natural events. In our craving for clarity, guidance, and foresight, we often interpret misfortune as divine punishment and good fortune as deserved blessings. For all the gifts nature offers and all the challenges it presents, nature is simply nature—neither fair nor unfair, punitive nor rewarding. It merely exists, independent of our interpretations and desires. As sentient beings of nature, we need to accept and adapt to whatever nature delivers and acknowledge that it operates indifferently to our desires or interpretations.

October 24

Mortality

Time is the currency of life. The challenge is: How much of this finite resource will you contribute to your life's journey, and how much can you afford to squander?

Time is life's most precious resource. It is finite and irreplaceable, demanding careful allocation. Before investing time, evaluate the potential return. Ask yourself: Will this yield meaningful value? Does it align with my goals?

Unlike material assets, time cannot be replenished. Use it judiciously. Avoid frivolous activities that drain this limited resource. Instead, focus on pursuits that promise growth, fulfillment, or progress toward your aspirations. Approach time management with intentionality. Expect worthwhile returns on your temporal investments, be it personal development, relationships, or goal achievement. Reconsider activities that don't meet this criterion. Invest your time wisely and purposefully, as each moment is irretrievable.

October 25

Emotion

Fear stares you in the face. Anxiety lurks in the back of your mind.

Fear is a visceral, immediate emotion that confronts us directly, demanding our attention and often prompting an instantaneous response. It manifests as a palpable presence, impossible to ignore, compelling us to face it head-on. Fear is facing the protective mother bear with two cubs on the trail with only one exit. Anxiety is a more insidious force. It operates in the shadows of our consciousness, a constant but often nebulous presence that gnaws at our peace of mind. Anxiety is what your mind dreams up when you hear an unknown sound in the forest and think you hear a menacing bear.

While fear presents itself boldly, anxiety subtly infiltrates our thoughts, creating a persistent undercurrent of unease that can be equally, if not more, debilitating. Both emotions serve as survival mechanisms, but their contrasting natures require different strategies for management and resolution. Recognize the immediacy of fear, and be prepared to protect and defend yourself. Acknowledge the intangibility of anxiety, and assess the risk and likelihood of the event. Your ability to differentiate between them and control your response will aid in your physical and emotional survival.

October 26

Awareness

Silent reflection gives rise to inner peace and wisdom.

Embrace the profound impact of silence, allowing its deafening presence to envelop you. In this quiet space, turn your attention inward and listen intently to the innermost workings of your mind and body. When the external noise is stripped away, you will be surprised to discover your internal world's richness, strength, and intensity. Silence serves as a powerful amplifier. It magnifies the subtle whispers of your thoughts, the rhythmic beats of your heart, and the gentle ebb and flow of your breath. This introspective journey through stillness can reveal hidden depths of your consciousness. It can unveil insights and awareness often drowned out by the cacophony of daily life. Cultivate a practice of intentional silence. Create opportunities for self-discovery, reflection, and rejuvenation. Allow your inner voice to resonate with clarity and purpose.

October 27

Social Thought

Enlightenment is the illuminating light of expansive knowledge.

Some seek spiritual enlightenment with little or no effort made to acquire self-awareness or intellectual knowledge. Yet, having a deep knowledge of oneself and an expansive knowledge of the world often culminates in or contributes to spiritual enlightenment. Conversely, a lack of self-awareness and worldly knowledge tends to hamper both spiritual enlightenment and self-actualization. By actively seeking enlightenment through acquiring knowledge, we expand our perspectives, challenge our preconceptions, and develop a more nuanced understanding of the world around us.

Cultivate an insatiable thirst for knowledge, both intellectual and spiritual. Driven by curiosity, relentlessly explore, question, and learn from diverse sources and experiences. Focus on not only acquiring but also understanding what you discover and experience. Make your quest for knowledge a lifelong journey, and you will grow ever wiser.

October 28

Action

We spend years learning how to speak but rarely take a single lesson in listening.

From childhood to advanced age, we commit considerable time, effort, and money to become proficient and eloquent in our speech. We hone our talent for articulating our thoughts clearly and succinctly. We seize moments to pontificate our opinions verbosely. We want everyone to hear, understand, and appreciate us and our ideas. Yet, we often neglect to grant others the courtesy we so deeply desire from them. We want to be heard, but we don't strive to hear others. We don't learn how to listen. This casts us in an imbalance of communication, which invariably leads to misunderstanding and mistrust. By neglecting to cultivate our listening skills, we risk becoming less proficient in engaging in conversation with and understanding the perspectives of others.

It would be best to turn off distractions, open our minds, close our mouths, and listen for once. Really listen.

October 29

Problem Solving

Civil opposition is a rational response to hypocrisy and to societal conventions that are no longer relevant.

Challenge hypocrisy with unwavering scrutiny, and question outdated societal norms. Boldly confront inconsistencies in beliefs and actions. Expose the flaws in hypocritical behavior that undermine integrity and social progress. Simultaneously, dare to challenge long-standing conventions that may have outlived their relevance or usefulness in our rapidly changing world. By critically examining and, when necessary, defying these established norms, we pave the way for innovative thinking and societal advancement. This encourages a dynamic, forward-thinking mindset that values authenticity and adaptability over blind adherence to tradition.

October 30

Resilience

Acknowledge others' opinions of you, but do not give them more value than warranted.

Recognizing how others perceive you can provide valuable insights, helping you grow and improve. However, it is essential to remember that these opinions are shaped by individual perspectives, biases, and limited understanding of your true self. While feedback can be constructive, allowing it to define your worth or dictate your choices can undermine your confidence and authenticity. Opinions should inform you, not control you. Reflect on what resonates with your values and discard what doesn't align. Stay grounded in your self-awareness, trusting your own judgment above the fleeting thoughts of others. Your path is yours to navigate.

October 31

Amor Fati

Life exists in appreciation of the moment, not in regret or hope.

Fully embrace the present moment, immersing yourself in the richness of now. Have a deep appreciation for the experiences, relationships, and opportunities that surround you today. Embrace the difficult and mundane moments along with the fulfilling and joyful ones. Resist the temptation to dwell on past regrets or to fixate on future fantasies. Instead, channel your focus onto the immediate reality before you. By living and loving wholeheartedly in the present, you open yourself to a more authentic and fulfilling existence, unburdened by the weight of what was or the uncertainty of what might be.

LAP AROUND THE SUN

November

November 1

Resilience

Those who demand allegiance and obedience have only their own interests in mind.

Blind discipline and blind loyalty require doing the bidding of others, without question and without regard to one's own thoughts, beliefs, and judgment. Such servile allegiance is often demanded and used by those in authority to manipulate others to serve their political, religious, or social fanaticism. In sharp contrast, purposeful discipline and intentional action involve applying one's own critical thinking to make logical decisions and take reasonable actions to achieve beneficial and tangible results.

Have a clear purpose in what you pursue and to whom you give your loyalty. Don't succumb to unthinking loyalty or blind ambition. Maintain independence in your goals, thoughts, actions, and commitments. Be guided by your intellect and intention and don't surrender them to the whims of others.

November 2

Emotion

Excessive worry and anxiety can plague anyone and benefit no one.

Worry is thinking about a genuine concern, while anxiety is ruminating about a perceived threat. When managed, worry and anxiety prompt us to take notice of and take action to mitigate potentially negative outcomes. Unmanaged worry or anxiety is when we continuously review the concern or threat in our minds, usually without effectively assessing or addressing it. Dwelling on what did or might happen doesn't alter the past or predestine the future. It merely causes distress and distracts us from the present, which can paralyze us or cripple our efforts to resolve the issue and relieve the stress.

If and when worry or anxiety creep up on you, acknowledge what you're feeling and why. Get clarity on exactly what you are concerned about and what, if anything, you can do to allay your concerns. Change what you can; let go of what you can't. Focus on what is in front of you now.

November 3

Awareness

Before finding faults in others, we should first reflect on our own.

It's remarkably easy to spot the flaws and shortcomings in others. These imperfections often seem so glaring that we wonder how they can't see and fix them themselves. But hold on: Why are we so quick to focus on others' faults rather than our own? Why do we eagerly gossip about these observations behind people's backs? Wouldn't our energy and perceptiveness be better directed toward self-assessment?

We all have faults—some apparent to us, others visible only to those around us. Everyone has room for improvement, but the first step is recognizing and acknowledging our own shortcomings, preferably before examining others. Challenge yourself to see yourself as others see you, rather than through your own biased lens. Don't be surprised if your reflection mirrors the imperfections you see in others.

November 4

Social Thought

It isn't about how much stuff you have; it's about what you do and why with what you have.

The accurate measure of one's worth isn't decided by the quantity or quality of possessions one accumulates, but rather by how effectively and meaningfully those possessions are used. Material wealth, while often coveted, is just a collection of objects. Stuff is just stuff. The real value lies in the purpose we assign to these items and the positive impact we can create with them. It's not the abundance of resources that defines us, but our ability to leverage what we have to make a difference in our lives and the lives of others. The significance of our possessions is not inherent in the objects themselves, but rather in the actions and intentions with which we apply them.

November 5

Action

Effective communication centers on listening to understand and speaking to be understood.

Communication is a complex, multi-faceted skill to master. Even the most casual conversation can turn sour on a single word, said or unsaid. Even benign or prudent statements and questions, if delivered at an inopportune time or in an appropriate tone or volume, can impede or implode a discussion. Prologued or utter silence can be alienating to other participants, while dominating the conversation can be off-putting.

You do not have to be the center of any conversation. It is often far better to be someone who listens attentively, assesses thoughtfully, and speaks judiciously rather than someone who chatters on about nothing. Listen to learn. Question to understand and to challenge, not to argue or discount. Speak clearly, calmly, and respectfully. Communicate with the intention to foster understanding, regardless of consensus, among the participants.

November 6

Mortality

Upon death, we part not only with our physical existence but also with our worldly possessions. Is our fear of death rooted in our fear of loss or the unknown?

Death, the universal human experience, raises a fundamental question: Is our fear of death primarily rooted in our attachment to possessions or in our apprehension of the mysterious unknown lying beyond? It's worth contemplating how our perspective might shift if we view the unknown not as a source of loss but as an opportunity for gain. Would this paradigm shift transform our apprehension into anticipation or even eagerness to face the unknown, not only in death but also throughout our lives?

This thought pushes us to more closely examine our relationship with material things. We often find ourselves desperately clinging to our possessions, even if it hinders our growth and future prospects. These self-imposed limits may prevent us from fully embracing our spiritual and personal evolution.

November 7

Problem Solving

To understand something in totality, it must be seen in its entirety and from every perspective.

Partial views of an idea, situation, observation, or problem can distort reality, leading to flawed assumptions and misguided actions. Understanding in totality means considering all perspectives, even those that challenge our own beliefs. It requires stepping outside our biases, asking deeper questions, and recognizing the broader context.

In problem solving, this approach is essential. Addressing only symptoms without exploring root causes or focusing solely on one viewpoint often leads to short-term fixes or new problems down the line. A full, well-rounded understanding reveals hidden connections and better paths forward. It encourages empathy, innovation, and long-term solutions.

To take action, commit to slowing down, gathering diverse input, and examining issues from multiple angles. Only then can decisions be both wise and effective. Let full understanding—not convenience—guide how you think, decide, and act.

November 8

Amor Fati

Today's choices influence tomorrow's outcomes.

Accepting fate is different from fatalism. Whereas fatalism suggests a predetermined and unchangeable future, accepting fate involves a realistic assessment of what we encounter. This perspective acknowledges that our destiny is not set in stone but rather is a malleable outcome shaped by our choices and actions. We craft it daily through our responses to the situations, challenges, and opportunities we meet. Accepting fate embraces the concepts of personal responsibility and the potential for growth and change despite seemingly insurmountable odds. With this capability, you can approach life's challenges with resilience, adaptability, and ownership with confidence, knowing that you are the architects of your own destiny.

November 9

Social Thought
Never confuse wealth with worth.

Wealth and worth are distinct concepts with little overlap. Throughout history, some of the wealthiest individuals have been among the least worthy. The unworthy wealthy are those who use their money and position primarily for self-benefit and to aid those who could advance their interests, showing little inclination toward selfless altruism. While it is commendable to work hard and accumulate enough wealth for comfort and security, a person's true value lies not in the amount of material wealth they've amassed but in how they've used their wealth.

The worthiest among us offer something far more precious than money: their time and energy. These individuals selflessly and tirelessly dedicate themselves to helping those less fortunate. If you are questioning someone's integrity, ask yourself if they are giving with the expectation of getting something in return. Those of worth do not expect a quid pro quo. Good people give from the goodness of their character.

November 10

Emotion

Decisions guided solely by emotions are often dangerous.

Typically, the more intense our emotions, the more impact they have on our behavior. The more rigid our thoughts and beliefs, the more impact they have on our emotions. Decisions and actions triggered by raw emotion pose considerable risks. Decisions and actions that don't consider the emotions associated with the situation also pose risks. Sound judgment derives from rational thought (unbiased by emotion) and emotional intelligence (emotion tempered with reason).

Cultivate emotional intelligence by endeavoring to recognize, understand, and regulate your emotions. Cultivate your power of reason by endeavoring to recognize, understand, and regulate your thoughts, beliefs, and perceptions. Before making a decision and acting on it, process your emotions and gather your thoughts. Consider your feelings, but lean into your intellect.

November 11

Awareness

Ego and self-deception are formidable obstacles on the path to personal growth and self-improvement.

Self-deception often results in overrating or underrating one's competencies, shortcomings, achievements, and failures. It forms a psychological barrier to perceiving oneself with a critical and discerning eye, leading to either an inflated or deflated ego—neither of which fosters personal growth and self-improvement. Both self-deception and a self-perception of superiority or inferiority have the potential not only to hinder progress but also to precipitate self-destructive patterns of behavior.

Self-awareness allows us to challenge our preconceptions and expand our horizons, pushing beyond our comfort zones to unlock new potential. This mindset gives us the power to resist the temptation to fall into either an entitled or victim mentality. Instead, we should take ownership of our abilities and experiences and use them as opportunities for growth and self-discovery. This empowers us to continuously evolve, learn, and adapt in the face of life's challenges.

Cultivate a sense of humility and open-mindedness. Recognize your perception of yourself, and acknowledge your capabilities and limitations, with the understanding that your assessment may be distorted or incomplete.

November 12

Mortality

The brocade of our existence is woven with threads of our mortal awareness intertwined with the vibrant-colored threads of our triumphs and the somber-hued threads of our setbacks.

Our consciousness of life's finite nature serves as the backdrop against which we paint our positive and negative experiences. Our perception of our mortality often acts as a catalyst, pushing us to strive for success and meaning in our limited time. True success is a complex pattern of our blessings and victories as well as the lessons learned from our struggles and failures. The journey toward genuine achievement requires us to face adversity, experiencing the sharp pangs of disappointment and mustering the strength to rise above those challenges. By confronting and overcoming obstacles, we develop resilience, wisdom, and a deeper appreciation for our accomplishments. Our acceptance of death and our experiences of success and failure are not separate elements but rather integral components of a rich, well-lived life.

November 13

Action

If you want to go far, take someone along. If you want to go fast, go alone.

The journey of personal growth and achievement often presents a choice between speed and distance. When one opts for rapid progress, solitude can be advantageous, allowing for quick decision-making and unimpeded action. However, this approach may limit the breadth and depth of one's experiences.

On the other hand, choosing to embark on a journey with companions may slow the pace, but it offers the potential for greater safety and the likelihood of success. Collaboration and shared experiences can lead to more comprehensive learning, diverse perspectives, and a more fulfilling and extensive journey. The companionship not only provides support and encouragement but it also challenges us to grow in ways we might not have anticipated when traveling alone.

While solitary efforts may yield swift results, the richness of a shared journey often proves more rewarding in the long run.

November 14

Problem Solving
Keep life simple. Good choices help.

Life, by nature, can be abusively complex. We often yearn for past times of our youth, when things were simpler, or for the times when our relationship with our parents or children were less complex. In the churn of incessantly doing and accumulating (things, experiences, relationships), we often crave and seek out the simple things in life. By consistently making thoughtful and beneficial choices, we can navigate the entanglements of our daily existence with greater ease and satisfaction. Prudent decisions act as steppingstones, guiding us toward a more streamlined and fulfilling lifestyle. Often, the tiny, seemingly insignificant choices accumulate to create significant positive change and to embrace simplicity in our lives.

November 15

Resilience
Take your life—not life's ups and downs—personally.

We all face both unfortunate, difficult events and uplifting, joyous ones. Life doesn't discriminate as humans do. It merely presents situations for us to experience. How those experiences affect us and how we respond to them is ours alone to determine. Whether life delivers a negative or positive situation to your life, the most effective approach to interpreting and reacting to the experience is from a place of self-awareness and authenticity.

Patiently embrace every experience, good or bad, and focus on being true to your core beliefs in both your choices and actions. Recognizing that your beliefs evolve with experience, allow yourself to grow as you face life's joys and tragedies. How you confront and address these situations will become part of you and aid you in your future. Be mindful of your actions and their consequences while keeping a passionate sense of purpose.

November 16

Amor Fati

Accept where you are, and set a plan to get to where you want to be.

It's impossible to chart a course for your future if you can't accept your current reality. Self-delusion and egocentrism often cloud our self-assessments. True self-awareness of both your positive and negative attributes demands brutal honesty; it's the only way to genuinely be yourself. This clear-eyed understanding provides a solid foundation, rooting you firmly in self-knowledge. From this vantage point, you can confidently set your future plans and aspirations.

Dream big and craft audacious goals. Don't hold back. Your one mortal life is brimming with potential for great achievements. The journey begins with accepting who and where you are today.

November 17

Awareness

Extreme repression often triggers extreme reaction. Push people too far, and they will rebel.

When people face severe suppression or oppression, they tend to eventually react strongly. Humans naturally crave autonomy, self-expression, civil rights, and dignity. Consistently denying those needs to someone can lead them to a breaking point. People will revolt when pushed too far. This highlights the need for governing pragmatically, communicating openly, and respecting individual freedoms to support social harmony and avoid upheaval.

November 18

Emotion

Magnified emotions magnify experiences and behavior, which degrades reason and reaction.

The importance of maintaining emotional control is especially evident during experiences that trigger our most powerful emotions: anger, fear, guilt, sadness, joy, love, gratitude, and empathy. These intense emotional states can amplify our reactions, compelling us to employ rash decisions and actions—often to the detriment of ourselves and/or others. When we allow our emotions to overpower our rational thinking, we become vulnerable to impulsive decisions and actions that may not serve our best interests. Moreover, in competitive or adversarial situations, an opponent can exploit these heightened emotional states to their advantage. Emotional resilience protects us from potential pitfalls and enables us to navigate difficult situations with greater acuity and self-control.

Recognize the impact of powerful emotions, particularly those you feel often and/or intensely. Consciously work to manage your emotions and assess the situation at hand. Maintain a clear perspective and your composure, and you will make more thoughtful choices.

November 19

Mortality

A shortened life doesn't mean we can't enjoy life. Make pausing an integral part of your journey and life tasks.

The finite nature of our existence should not deter us from savoring life's simple pleasures, even when the potential for spectacular experiences has passed. While we may be acutely aware of our mortality, it's important to also be aware that life's journey holds immense value in and of itself. By intentionally incorporating moments of pause and reflection into our daily lives, we enrich our experiences and deepen our appreciation for the world around us. Whether spent in quiet contemplation or joyful engagement with our surroundings and loved ones, these brief interludes become an essential part of our life's narrative. They offer us opportunities to recharge, gain perspective, and find meaning in the seemingly mundane aspects of our existence. Through this engagement with and appreciation for the fundamental riches of life, we enhance our well-being and cultivate a greater sense of purpose and fulfillment.

November 20

Social Thought

I don't know what you don't know, nor do I know what I don't know. But I do know the more I know, the more I know I don't know.

You cannot presume to know the extent of another person's understanding or misunderstanding or to fully grasp the boundaries of your own ignorance. However, with each new piece of information acquired, you become increasingly aware of the immense expanse of knowledge that still lies beyond your comprehension. This paradox of learning—where increased knowledge leads to a greater recognition of one's own limitations—is as humbling as it is inspiring. It drives us to continually seek additional information, question our assumptions, and approach the world with wonder and curiosity. The more we learn, the more we realize how much there is yet to discover, creating an endless cycle of growth and intellectual exploration.

November 21

Action

Because life is a series of small events spiked with rare spectacular moments, you can achieve remarkable things by conquering each small opportunity.

Life unfolds as a stream of countless, seemingly insignificant experiences highlighted with rare moments of extraordinary significance. This pattern offers us the opportunity to achieve greatness not through grand, sweeping gestures but through the diligent mastery of each minor challenge and fleeting opportunity that presents itself. Facing these inconsequential instances with dedication and mindfulness, we can gradually build the foundation for remarkable accomplishments. We pave the way for those scarce but spectacular moments to manifest through the accumulation of these small victories and defeats. True greatness often results from consistently seizing and maximizing the potential within life's everyday occurrences.

November 22

Problem Solving

The only thing you own is your time, as finite as it might be. The only things you control are how you manage your time and your reactions to events in your life.

Time is our most precious possession, and our actions are our sole domain of control. Every point along each of our laps around the sun is invaluable and unrepeatable, even the seemingly ordinary. It's up to us to imbue these moments with significance. Our time is finite, but it's ours to manage. How we use it through our actions is truly the only thing we control. External factors, be they natural or human, inevitably influence our reactions, yet we are still responsible for our responses. Even when we allow these external forces to guide us, the choice to allow that is our own. Strive to use your time wisely, contributing positively to society while keeping your integrity and purpose in every action you take.

November 23

Resilience

Independent thinking is the strongest defense against coercion and the strongest catalyst of liberation.

Barring brain disease and dementia, nothing and nobody can mold, control, or change what we think ... unless we allow it. A healthy brain and mind provide us with the capacity to form, process, and manage our individual perceptions, thoughts, and beliefs—regardless of what others think and might try to force upon us. This free mind empowers us to choose our perceptions and reactions, even in the face of adversity. It grants us an unyielding intellectual strength that shields us from the attempts of tormentors, manipulators, and influencers seeking to control our thinking to do their bidding. Do what you must, but don't succumb to their invasive and persuasive tactics. Hold fast to what is yours: your strong, free mind.

November 24

Amor Fati

Negative, fearful perspectives can become a self-created prison.

When our minds are dominated by fearful or negative thoughts, we develop negative mindsets that darken our perspectives and dampen our spirits. Left unchecked, these pessimistic viewpoints and attitudes become fixed, creating a cognitive prison that limits our potential, hinders our growth, and sabotages our happiness. Breaking free from this mental confinement lies in our ability to acknowledge and shift our mindsets and attitude toward any given circumstance.

Just as we are powerless to change the direction of the wind or redirect the course of a mighty river, so too are we powerless to change the situations we face. However, we possess complete authority over our interpretations of and reactions to these events.

Rather than futilely trying to alter external factors beyond your control, try to accept them as they are. Avoid self-sabotage by changing your attitude toward any adverse circumstance. Consciously choose to adopt a more positive and constructive mindset to navigate life's challenges with greater resilience and optimism. Focus on acknowledging and transforming your internal landscape—your thoughts, beliefs, attitudes, and actions associated with the situation.

November 25

Mortality

Nothing is meant to be; predestination is a myth

The concept of predestination is the idea that events are predetermined or destined to happen. Many find this notion comforting, while others find it disquieting. Regardless of how predestination is interpreted, it is a concept that lacks empirical support. Our lives are not scripted in advance. Rather, our lives unfold through a complex interplay of choices, circumstances, chance, and chaos.

The absence of a predetermined path offers both freedom and responsibility. We are the authors of our own stories, shaping our futures through our decisions and actions. While external factors certainly influence our journey, the absence of predestination empowers us to actively take part in creating our own destiny. This supports personal growth, resilience, and adaptability in the face of life's unpredictable nature.

It is worth repeating: there is no celestial puppet master; nothing is predetermined or predestined. Envision and create your own destiny.

November 26

Emotion

Evil is rooted in hate, unbridled lust, and fallacy.

Hatred, a powerful negative emotion, can drive individuals to commit heinous acts against others, fueled by a combination of prejudice, anger, or desire for revenge. *Lust*, when unchecked and allowed to consume one's thoughts and actions, can lead to the objectification and exploitation of others, disregarding their humanity and dignity. *Fallacy*, fantasized or erroneous thoughts, manifests as a distorted perception of reality, often resulting in misguided beliefs and actions that can harm both the individual and those around them. These three elements often intertwine with and reinforce each other, creating a toxic foundation from which evil intentions and deeds spring forth, corrupting the human spirit and causing untold suffering.

To counteract these destructive forces, turn inward and cultivate self-awareness and reflection. By confronting our own negative emotions and biases, we can better understand their roots and avoid projecting them onto others. Striving for empathy, self-control, and critical thinking allows us to break free from harmful patterns and builds a foundation of respect, dignity, and understanding, thereby preventing the harmful cycle of destructive behavior.

November 27

Awareness

If you aren't humbled when you watch the differently-abled just live life, you have no mind and are dead inside.

It is disheartening how often we take everyday life for granted. We fret over trivial inconveniences and obstacles, constantly wishing for an easier existence. Our egocentrism blinds us to those who overcome far more significant challenges to simply live their lives and to achieve common as well as remarkable successes. The athletes of the Paralympics, for example, should fill us with awe. Even more humbling are the everyday accomplishments of people with physical, and mental disabilities. Our daily struggles pale in comparison, making our complaints seem petty. People who are unmoved by the efforts and achievements of people with disabilities have lost touch with their humanity and compassion.

To foster gratitude and compassion, we should become more aware of the challenges faced by individuals with disabilities. Rather than fixating on minor inconveniences, let's recognize the strength and resilience required to navigate life with physical and mental disabilities. By acknowledging the accomplishments of people with disabilities, we can shift our perspectives. Being more conscientious in our views means valuing their humanity, challenging preconceived notions, and cultivating a deeper sense of empathy and respect for their experiences.

November 28

Social Thought

Only the fragile and shallow play the martyr, always looking for scapegoats to blame for their choices and actions.

Deflecting blame onto others and portraying oneself as a victim can be a powerful tool in swaying those who are already loyal or easily influenced. This approach may prove sufficient if your adversary cannot effectively mobilize those with more discerning and realistic perspectives. It is important to note while this tactic may yield short-term gains, it often comes at the cost of credibility and can potentially backfire if overused or exposed. The effectiveness of such a strategy depends on the context, the audience's critical thinking skills, and the opponent's ability to present a compelling counter-narrative that appeals to more objective observers.

To avoid falling into the trap of deflecting blame and playing the victim, focus on accountability and integrity in your actions and words. Blaming others offers only temporary relief, and it ultimately erodes trust and credibility. Instead, engage in honest self-reflection and address issues directly. Short-term gains from playing the martyr are easily undone, whereas personal accountability yields resiliency.

November 29

Action

Our greatest strength is unconditional kindness.

Sincere kindness, our most potent and enduring strength, stands as an impenetrable fortress against the assaults of meanness, rudeness, cruelty, and hate. These negative traits often serve as a thin veil, masking a fundamental weakness within those who wield them. Their unkind actions often stem from insecurity or vulnerability. The frailty of their ideas, positions, and character inevitably manifests itself in various forms of cruelty. These bullies often try to compensate for their lack of inner strength through aggression or malice. In contrast, genuine kindness emanates from inner fortitude and self-assurance, requiring no external validation or the diminishment of others to thrive.

When you encounter individuals who resort to such behaviors, let your actions reflect the quite strength of sincere kindness. In the face of cruelty, respond with grace –not to appease but to stand firm in your personal integrity. Aggression masks insecurity, choose not to mirror it. Instead, ground yourself in compassion, speak with empathy, and let kindness be your unwavering standard.

November 30

Problem Solving

The greatest leaders recognize and give precedence to the greater good, not corrupt self-interest

---

Strong, effective leadership prioritizes collective interests over personal gain and eschews corrupt or skewed influences and judgments. This demands self-awareness and discerning reflection, and it allows leaders to see beyond self-interest and gain a holistic view of challenges and opportunities. Leaders who remain insightful, unbiased, and steady build trust and security. True leadership transcends personal ambition, embracing a higher purpose to elevate others for the common good.

Lead for the greater good, not your self-interest, even if you believe your self-interest aligns with the common good. Seek out and support leaders who embody this as well. Leadership isn't limited to titles; it lives in everyday choices. Whether or not you see yourself as a leader, you influence others through your integrity, awareness, and fairness. Resist the pull of self-interest or bias; instead, act with clarity and purpose. When you prioritize the greater good over personal gain, you quietly embody the kind of leadership that builds trust, uplifts others, and creates lasting impact.

December

December 1

Resilience

Beware of the misguided influence and malicious intent of others.

It is within our control to prevent or halt fools and scoundrels from negatively influencing and impacting our lives. That control, however, requires paying attention to their behavior, running it through our internal truth detector, and either rejecting, opposing, or simply ignoring them.

Use your powers of observation and discernment to recognize and accept such buffoons and thugs for who and what they are. Consider their hidden agendas and the roles they play. Recognize, but do not indulge these bad actors and/or agendas. Don't follow or be fooled by them, and don't lose your direction or perspective in the flurry of lies, distractions, and obstructions they create. Keep calm, keep your head, and keep your focus on what matters most to you. These misguided or malicious influencers will continue their ranting until they realize their tactics are not affecting you and move on to their next target.

December 2

Amor Fati

We can't change the past, but we can shape our future from this moment on.

The past is gone forever, irrefutable and irreversible. Dwelling on the past and wishing or thinking we could alter it is futile. Looking backward is helpful only for learning from past experiences in order to change our future trajectory. No matter how small or significant, our actions today will inevitably shape the landscape of our tomorrows, starting right now.

As each day passes, it swiftly becomes a part of your personal history. Rather than dwelling on your past, acknowledge and accept it for what it is and where it has brought you. Look to the present for the promise of tomorrow, which is ever-present, beckoning you with endless possibilities and opportunities for growth and transformation. Today soon becomes the past, and tomorrow is forever, always ahead and forward.

December 3

Mortality

Throughout life's journey, the river of life carves its unique path, shaping the landscape it traverses and leaving behind a legacy in its wake.

Life is like a river, with a trickling start at its headwaters that flows through the expanding and turbulent waters of adolescence, the swift currents and restful eddies of adulthood, and the languid melancholy of advanced age before entering the vast ocean of everlasting peace. Never underestimate the power of your life's journey and the indelible marks you've left along the way. Your legacy of knowledge and experiences will be viewed and admired by many—guiding the lost, invigorating the discouraged, calming the distressed, and buoying the weary. On and on your legacy will be passed along, joining the great body of wisdom upon which future lives will be based—never ceasing, never forgotten.

December 4

Emotion

Anger exhibits weakness and lack of self-control, not strength and composure.

Anger shows a loss of emotional equilibrium. This loss of control diminishes our ability to reason clearly and often leads to regrettable actions and words. When we succumb to anger, we expose our inability to effectively manage our emotions and often our actions. This highlights a vulnerability rather than power. Real strength lies in keeping equanimity in the face of provocation. Those who can remain calm and collected in challenging situations exhibit genuine strength of character and emotional intelligence. These traits are far more admirable and effective in navigating life's complexities.

December 5

Awareness

Everyone deserves the benefit of the doubt and a chance to earn the respect of others.

Upon our first encounter with someone, we all desire to be treated with respect. Whether our history is a burden or a crown, we don't want our past to define us. We want to be seen for who and all that we are now. Each of us, in our own way, looks for and deserves the benefit of doubt. With every new interaction, we all hope for the opportunity to build a relationship based on mutual understanding and acceptance. We should extend this trust and respect to everyone, until and unless they prove unworthy of it. Even then, if someone falters, we should pause to consider their circumstances. Under certain conditions, any of us might also stumble. In the end, it's far better to be accepting and accepted than to withhold understanding and misjudge one another.

December 6

Social Thought

Whether something is "good" or "bad" is a personal judgment that is subject to change.

The concepts of good and bad are inherently intertwined. They exist as contrasting opinions rather than absolute truths. What one person perceives as good may be viewed as bad from another's perspective, and vice versa. A person's take on whether something or someone is good or bad reflects their individual mindsets, beliefs, and choices. The relativity of these concepts highlights the subjective nature of moral judgments and ethical considerations. Neither good nor bad exist as an objective reality except in the most egregious of human behavior.

Good and bad are mental constructs shaped by our cultural backgrounds, personal experiences, and interpretations of the world around us. As our understanding evolves and circumstances change, so too can our perceptions of good and bad change. This fluidity underscores the importance of open-mindedness and a willingness to reconsider our standpoints as we consider unfamiliar information or differing viewpoints.

December 7

Action

Present yourself, live your life, and assess others through mindful actions rather than merely comforting words.

Words can be deceiving. Actions reveal true character and intent. While well-intentioned, the oft-used phrase "thoughts and prayers" rings hollow and falls short in comparison with objective assessment and corrective action. Real change and progress come from decisive deeds that address issues head-on. While empathy and support expressed through words have their place, the concrete steps we take to improve situations, solve problems, and help others are more tangibly effective in the world. Only through our actions can we create meaningful impact and lasting change.

December 8

Problem Solving

When we listen attentively before joining a conversation, we speak more perceptively and are more likely to be heard.

We often prefer to hear ourselves talk, eagerly sharing our ideas and opinions before others. However, this tendency causes us to miss out on the rich resource of others' perspectives. By listening before expressing ourselves and giving our full attention to whoever is speaking, we gain from their experiences and intellect. This approach also prepares us to ask relevant questions and contribute valid perspectives. This creates a broader foundation for problem solving.

In a discussion, make a conscious effort to listen until all or most of the other participants have been heard before offering your thoughts. Listen to comprehend, not merely to formulate a reply. Speak to foster understanding, not to argue or defend your point of view. Wait until the person talking is finished speaking to ask questions or share your thoughts, and expect the same courtesy in return. Be willing to listen first and talk last, allowing everyone else to speak their piece before speaking yours. By listening first, you will learn more, influence more effectively, and solve problems more successfully.

December 9

Resilience

The poetry of your life is crafted each moment of every day from your desires, disappointments, perceptions, and experiences.

Every day, create the intricate verses of your life's poem with vision, determination, understanding, and compassion. Infuse them with your aspirations and unwavering resilience. Let your determination be the rhythm that propels you forward as insight forms the beat of your interactions. Incorporate compassion into every line, creating a song of experiences that reflects your inner strength and empathy. With each passing movement, add new stanzas to your personal epic, blending the raw emotions of toughness with the gentle cadence of kindness. This daily composition, rich in depth and nuance, will form the masterpiece of your existence—a testament to the artistry of living with purpose and heart.

December 10

Amor Fati

Differences and disagreements are inevitable. But they need not be barriers to acceptance, solidarity, and betterment.

In the grand collage of human existence, we find ourselves blended through the commonality of diversity. Some individuals are blessed with abundance, while others struggle with scarcity. Our beliefs span a wide spectrum—from conservative to liberal, religious to atheist, optimistic to pessimistic, stoic to hysteric, and everything in between. Despite these clear differences, we all share a common truth: our time in this world is finite and precious.

It's time we shift our focus away from scrutinizing our trivial differences and toward our commonalities. Instead of dwelling on what sets us apart, we could embrace a more accepting mindset. Instead of concentrating on what we have or don't have, like or don't like, we could channel our energy into a collective effort to enhance the quality of life for all. We could set aside our judgments and foster understanding and acceptance. We could open ourselves to the possibility of creating a more harmonious and virtuous world for all during our life's brief sojourn. Isn't leaving the world a better place the noblest pursuit we can undertake in our limited time? It's worth a try, even if we disagree on what a better world looks like.

December 11

Social Thought

Philosophy guides us through morality, nature, and reason—shaping a life of clarity, balance, and purpose.

Philosophy offers a tripartite framework to help chart a life's course: moral, natural, and rational. Each part serves a distinct yet interconnected purpose in guiding our lives.

Morality acts as a compass for the soul. It helps us discern right from wrong and shapes our ethical landscape. It provides the foundation for our values and principles. It influences our decisions and actions in both personal and societal contexts.

The natural part encourages us to observe and understand the inherent order of the universe. It prompts us to explore the fundamental governing laws of nature. It helps foster a deeper appreciation for the intricate balance of our place in the holistic world.

Rationality gives us the tools that help us make sense of life's myriad experiences and challenges. It hones our critical thinking skills. It aids in our ability to analyze complex situations, draw logical conclusions, and support a healthy skepticism that keeps falsehoods and misconceptions at bay.

Together, these three pillars of philosophy form a comprehensive doctrine that empowers us to lead more thoughtful, balanced, and enriched lives.

December 12

Emotion

Anger, despair, and hate are choices. So are kindness, hope, and love.

When we keep our emotions in check and allow our minds and experiences to guide us, we maintain the power of choice. We have opportunities to decide which emotions we allow ourselves to experience and to what degree. We can opt to regulate negative emotions by noticing when we feel them arise, examining the experience and thoughts behind the emotion, and choosing whether to hold on to it or let it go. The choice is always ours to respond from a place of kindness, hope, and love or a place of anger, despair, and hate. These emotional responses aren't thrust upon us; we actively choose them. By controlling our reactions and emotions, we can make wiser choices that align with our best selves.

December 13

Awareness

Nature accepts all, because everything has a place in nature.

Humans often work under the misguided belief that we possess an inherent right to exert control over our environment and fellow beings. We try to alienate what we deem undesirable. We try to assimilate what we consider valuable. We try to control what we believe requires our intervention. However, this approach often leads to imbalance and conflict in our societies and in our relationship with the natural world.

A more harmonious approach would be to emulate nature's accepting stance. Rather than imposing our will upon others or our surroundings, we should allow every person, creature, and element on Earth to find its natural place. Concurrently, we should focus on discovering our legitimate position within this intricate web of existence. If we do, we can foster a more balanced, respectful, and sustainable way of living that aligns more closely with the natural order of things.

December 14

Social Thought
Over time, romantic love evolves into a devoted partnership.

New love brings excitement and apprehension. It boils with passion and enthralls with the discovery of the unknown. Mature love runs deeper. Passion evolves into a deep intimacy, and the couple's profound bond partner that elevates in importance. Mature love has weathered years of trials. It bears the physical and emotional scars from countless tests and reconciliations. Mature love is sustained by commitment, companionship, affection, and trust. It is accepting of a partner's changes, patient in its responses, and most importantly, selfless in its devotion to one another. Mature love puts your life's soulmate first, no matter what, when, or where.

December 15

Action

Discretion is the art of knowing whether, when, and how best to speak up or take action.

While eloquent speech has its place, the impact of consistent, resolute action can be far more profound and lasting. In other situations, strategic inaction and thoughtful silence can be more powerful than hasty action or speech. Refraining from immediate action or comment often provides opportunities for deeper reflection. This allows for more measured and effective responses when the time is right.

Gauge whether and when to intervene, speak up, or hold back. Let your deeds speak louder than your voice—be seen doing rather than heard talking. Let your actions demonstrate your commitment and values through tangible efforts. Balancing considered restraint with mindful engagement, you develop a commanding presence that secures respect and influences positive change.

December 16

Problem Solving
It is possible for vehemently opposed factions to resolve their differences amicably.

Opposites need not be antagonistic or in constant conflict. They may initially be at odds, but their relationship with one another is often more nuanced and dynamic. The natural tendency of opposing forces is to create tension and movement. They swing back and forth between one extreme and the other. This oscillation is not endless or necessarily destructive. Instead, it often leads to a process of concession, resolution, and equilibrium.

The stabilization toward a middle ground is not a sign of defeat, but rather a natural mechanism for preservation and sustainability. It is a harmonious coexistence in which the strengths of both sides are maintained, without the destructive aspects of extremism. Understanding this process can lead to more nuanced problem-solving and a greater appreciation for the complex and complementary nature of opposing ideas.

December 17

Resilience

Not every issue is yours to address or remedy.

There's a profound sense of liberation and contentment in abstaining from forming opinions on matters beyond our control or complete understanding. By consciously choosing not to have a stance on every issue, we liberate ourselves from unnecessary mental burdens and emotional entanglements. Selective engagement allows us to focus our energy and attention on areas in which we can genuinely have influence.

This doesn't mean ignoring key issues. Rather, it involves acknowledging our limitations and choosing where to invest our mental and emotional resources. It is a practice in mindfulness and self-awareness. It is recognizing the boundaries of our influence and finding contentment in that recognition. In this way, we create space for more meaningful pursuits and reduce the stress associated with feeling compelled to have an opinion on everything.

You can find real satisfaction in not having an opinion. Make things you don't control, influence, or fully understand irrelevant in your mind.

December 18

Amor Fati

What we do today determines our tomorrow.

Our past experiences and choices shape our present circumstances. Each decision we make and every step we take today sets in motion a series of events that will shape our tomorrow. The experienced moment instantly becomes part of our history. And so the cycle continues: the past shapes the present, the present shapes the future, and immediately becomes the past. Yet, the unwritten future holds no sway over how we act now. This underscores the criticality of our present actions. This forces us to understand that we are the architects of our destiny. Actions we undertake today not only impact the present, but they also serve as the foundations of our future.

December 19

Mortality

When you look at a window, do you gaze at your own reflection or view the world?

A window serves as both a mirror and a portal, offering two distinct vantage points. One view is egocentric, the other altruistic. In the mirror view, we see ourselves. We see our immediate concerns, personal reflections, and self-perceptions. In the portal view, we see the vast expanse of the world around us. We witness its complexities, opportunities, and the lives of others. We are inherently part of both perspectives. We often unconsciously prioritize one over the other. This choice significantly influences how we interact with and understand our place within our surroundings and society. Become aware of this choice. Gain the power to consciously decide where to direct attention. Learn to balance self-awareness with a broader worldview. We are children of the world, not the center of it.

December 20

Emotion

Learn from the past. Make the most of today. Look forward to the future.

Three general periods of time exist: past, present, and future. Dwelling on the past often romanticizes it, conveniently forgetting its harshness and struggles. Focusing solely on the present is shortsighted, risking the repetition of historical mistakes and missed future opportunities. Fixating on the future entraps us in the realm of unsupported dreams, leading to unrealistic expectations. Without grounding our perspective in all three periods, we will struggle to keep an unclouded vision of any of them. A balanced outlook acknowledges lessons from the past, embraces present realities, and anticipates future possibilities. This approach enables us to effectively navigate life's complexities and yields a solid foundation.

December 21

Awareness

Winning at all costs can be a catastrophic defeat.

In reality, many so-called victories are defeats, and many who believe themselves to be winners are losers—due to the cost or means by which they are acquired. Such victors assume the cost and means of any victory is worthwhile, regardless of loss of life, reputation, or value. Many who are viewed by others or see themselves as winners are suffering personal, financial, and ethical losses that could lead or have led to their downfall. Some victories are so horrific, so pyrrhic, that they are truly colossal defeats when viewed in terms of gain versus loss. The juxtaposition of winning and losing must be viewed relative to long-term consequences and morality.

True victory isn't measured by immediate gain; it is measured by the integrity of the path taken and the lasting impact left behind. Before attempting the struggle, ask yourself: Does the end warrant the means? Success should never come at the cost of your character. Let conscience, not ego, define what it means to win.

December 22

Mortality

As we emerge from a dark time in our lives, the days begin to get brighter and illuminate the path forward.

Today at dawn, we emerge from the winter solstice, knowing each new day will bring more light. This astronomical event signifies that we have transcended the longest, darkest night of the year, a metaphor that resonates profoundly with life's journey. When we face our darkest moments and persevere, we can take solace in the knowledge that we have endured and survived the worst. This realization becomes a source of strength, reminding us that we have the resilience to weather life's storms.

With each challenge surmounted, we gain confidence to move forward. Like the gradually lengthening days post-solstice, the path ahead promises increasing light and opportunity. Surviving our personal "darkest days" proves to us that we have the inner fortitude to face whatever lies ahead, armed with the wisdom gained from our experiences and the hope inspired by brighter days to come.

December 23

Action

Habits are not entrenched. Habits are our creations, and we can break or change them at will.

Habits are universal yet diverse. Some we consciously cultivate, while others evolve into personal quirks. Good habits can make life better or easier, while bad habits can lead to problems of disaster. However, even good habits can lull us into a false sense of security, encouraging repetitive and thoughtless actions. When we become oblivious to and overly reliant on our habitual behavior, we risk losing focus and defaulting to muscle memory. Problem-solving and ingenuity come from mental agility and intention, not muscle memory. So, it is crucial to examine and reassess our subconscious habits. We should avoid performing many actions, including loving or hating, out of mere habit. Even routine tasks deserve mindful execution. Instead, we should constantly seek improvement, rejecting the "that's how I've always done it" mentality. Embrace deliberation, purpose, thoughtfulness, and curiosity. There's always room for enhancement. We just have to keep searching for or innovating new solutions.

December 24

Problem Solving

Every goal achieved began with a dream of what might be.

Dreams should be boundless, unrestricted by self-imposed limitations or the constraints of today's reality. In the realm of imagination, we have the freedom to envision grand possibilities. We can explore the furthest reaches of our potential and conceive ideas that may seem impossible in in our present reality. Dreaming serves as a wellspring of creativity, inspiration, and motivation. It allows us to push beyond perceived boundaries, challenge conventional wisdom, and aspire to achievements that might otherwise seem out of reach. Many of humanity's greatest accomplishments began as seemingly impossible dreams. Let your imagination soar without restraint. In the limitless expanse of your dreams lies the seeds of future realities. If you can dream it, you or someone else can eventually achieve it.

December 25

Resilience

Regretting the past or fretting over the future burns energy you could use for what's in front of you now.

Expending mental, emotional, and physical energy on regrets about past events or anxieties burns energy you could use for what's in front of you today. When we fixate on what has already happened or might happen, we rob ourselves of the ability to act effectively in the here and now. Channeling our energy toward the tasks, relationships, and experiences currently within our sphere of influence allows us to make meaningful progress, solve pressing problems, and create positive change in our immediate circumstances. Redirecting our attention and efforts to the present maximizes our potential for growth and fulfillment.

The present is based on the irreversible past, and the future is based on today's actions. Pay attention to what you are doing today.

December 26

Amor Fati

Understanding of all things comes from understanding yourself.

Each of us has an innate capacity to discern truth and resist evil. This inner wisdom negates the need for external rituals or symbolic devotion. Self-knowledge and self-reliance are the cornerstones of understanding not just of ourselves, but of the world at large. The journey to understand the complexities of existence begins with introspection and self-knowledge. Turn your attention and fortify your self-awareness. Seek knowledge independent of external influences, and develop a profound trust in your judgment. This internal exploration serves as a compass that will guide you through the intricacies of morality and ethics without reliance on doctrines or institutions.

December 27

Mortality

Your time to accomplish, create, and influence is limited and precious.

At the close of every day, you are one step closer to finishing another lap around the sun. One day further from your birth and one day closer to your death. You have spent twenty-four hours of the precious, limited resource of your time. Your remaining time, however long, is now shorter. Your time to love, dream, build, teach, lead, mentor, and so much more is one day less. As you reflect on the passing day, did you fill it to its fullest? Did you set the stage for tomorrow and tomorrow's tomorrow? Your lifetime is not predetermined, but it is limited. Use your precious time wisely.

December 28

Emotion

Just as unregulated emotions can consume you, so too can unbridled power.

Power—the ability or capacity to influence, compel, or regulate others—is a force that demands careful mastery and control. Like a double-edged sword, it has the potential to empower or destroy. Without proper management, the allure of power can overwhelm one's judgment. This will lead to detrimental consequences. Develop the ability to wield power responsibly, balancing assertiveness with thoughtfulness and restraint. Through self-awareness and emotional intelligence, harness the positive aspects of power while mitigating its potential for harm. Enduring strength lies in the wisdom to use power sparingly and ethically, and to recognize when you cannot—and then have the moral strength to relinquish it.

December 29

Awareness

Nothing is destined or immutable. Everything is what it is and what we perceive it to be.

Sadness and joy abound in every life, affecting the wise, the spiritual, and the rogue without prejudice. Spirituality neither guarantees happiness nor shields against sorrow. Those who follow their own path toward enlightenment and self-awareness recognize happiness and sorrow for what they are: emotional responses to what's going on within and around them. These clear-minded, visionary fellow travelers have learned to treat both emotions with equal detachment. They understand that joy and sorrow are fleeting and that neither are preordained. They also understand that desire for joy and aversion to sadness often causes anxiety. The pursuit of happiness and the avoidance of sorrow create a circular pattern of thought, emotion, and behavior that benefits no one.

Accept and appreciate what surrounds you and comes your way—without classifying it as good or bad, reward or punishment, blessing or curse. Be aware of what brings you joy and sadness, but guard against overthinking or overrating your feelings. Embrace happiness and sorrow, but don't cling to either.

December 30

Social Thought

Be content with who you are, and strive to improve what you can.

Comparisons are part of nature. Although we would probably be better off avoiding comparisons, they are an unavoidable aspect of our lives. One of the most common things we compare is ourselves with others, even though it tends to cause more harm than good.

Being an average person is often undervalued in a culture obsessed with excellence and extremes. Yet, to be average is to reflect the natural rhythm of life—strong in some areas, weaker in others, and grounded in a realistic view of oneself. Unlike being average at all things, which implies uniformity without distinction, being an average person means embracing your individuality within a shared human experience. It allows for both growth and acceptance, reminding us that we don't need to be exceptional to live meaningful lives.

Striving for greatness in everything can lead to burnout, while embracing your average self can foster peace, authenticity, and resilience. Life isn't about outperforming others—it's about being grounded, honest, and present. So live your life embracing who you are, working to grow where it matters, and finding fulfillment not in standing out, but in showing up with sincerity and purpose. Simply, always do your best and recognize that is a life well-lived.

December 31

Action

Champions don't cry foul or take victory laps. They step back on the line, take on all comers, and start again.

On this eve of a new year, there is a strong tendency to look back on this past year and either cheer or cry. As you cross the finish line, release the death grip of the past and move forward. The choices you've made and steps you've taken have already laid the foundation for and set in motion a series of events that will shape your journey ahead. Glorifying or castigating bygone days serves little purpose.

Dwelling on and attempting to rectify past mistakes or deficiencies can sometimes lead to further complications. Free yourself to embrace new challenges without the burden of regret or the temptation to constantly revisit and "fix" what has already happened. Likewise, constantly replaying or attempting to replicate past victories can sometimes lead to missed opportunities. Often, the wisest course of action is to acknowledge, learn from, and then let go of past defeats and victories.

Your next Lap Around the Sun is about to begin. Let's get ready, and let's go! And Remember: Never Fear the Dream......

About the Author

William C. Barron is a published author of numerous technical articles and a regular guest columnist in regional news outlets. His blog, *simplebender.com*, has garnered an international readership across the United States, Canada, Europe, and Asia.

Graduating from The University of Texas and now a retired petroleum engineer, William brings decades of global experience, having worked professionally on three continents—above the Arctic Circle and below the Equator. His career has spanned roles from offshore roustabout to engineer, operations manager, and senior corporate executive. He also served as Director of the Oil and Gas Division for the State of Alaska. Currently, he is the Principal of Trispectrum Consulting. He is a co-holder of several patents and has provided expert testimony before state legislatures and at numerous public forums.

Outside of his professional achievements, William is a seasoned endurance athlete. He has represented Team USA at multiple ITU Duathlon World Championships, completed the Boston Marathon, and finished numerous half-Ironman and Ironman events.

Let's Go Around, Again

Thank you very much for taking time each day to read this book and take a Lap Around the Sun with me. It has been a pleasure sharing my thoughts as we delved into some subjects and ideas which might have been uncomfortable or clarifying.

If you enjoyed, were challenged, laughed, and even scoffed at some of the passages, then we had a good journey. If you would like to continue with some of these concepts and discussion events affecting all of us, you can do so at *simplebender.com*. There, you will find weekly articles entitled **'Never Fear the Dream'** and other more thoughtful articles. I'm always open to questions, comments, and suggestions and will always endeavor to reply promptly.

Thanks again….See you soon at *simplebender.com*…until then be the Champion your are and step back up on the line and let's go for another Lap.

Index

Action:

Jan-6, Jan-14, Jan-22, Jan-30,
  Feb-7, Feb-15, Feb-23,
  Mar-2, Mar-10, Mar-18, Mar-26,
  Apr-3, Apr-11, Apr-19, Apr-27,
  May-5, May-13, May-21, May-29,
  Jun-6, Jun-14, Jun-22, Jun-30,
  Jul-8, Jul-16, Jul-24,
  Aug-1, Aug-9, Aug-17, Aug-25,
  Sep-10, Sep-18, Sep-26,
  Oct-4, Oct-12, Oct-20, Oct-28,
  Nov-5, Nov-13, Nov-21, Nov-29,
  Dec-7, Dec-15, Dec-23, Dec-31

Amor Fati:

Jan-1, Jan-9, Jan-17, Jan-25,
  Feb-2, Feb-10, Feb-18, Feb-26,
  Mar-5, Mar-13, Mar-21, Mar-29,
  Apr-6, Apr-14, Apr-22, Apr-30,
  May-8, May-16, May-24,
  Jun-1, Jun-9, Jun-17, Jun-25,
  Jul-3, Jul-11, Jul-19, Jul-27,
  Aug-4, Aug-12, Aug-20, Aug-28,
  Sep-5, Sep-13, Sep-21, Sep-29,
  Oct-7, Oct-15, Oct-23, Oct-31,
  Nov-8, Nov-16, Nov-24, Dec-2,
  Dec-10, Dec-18, Dec-26

Awareness:

Jan-4, Jan-12, Jan-12, Jan-20, Jan-28,
Feb-5, Feb-13, Feb-21, Feb-29,
Mar-8, Mar-16, Mar-24,
Apr-1, Apr-9, Apr-17, Apr-25,
May-3, May-11, May-19, May-27,
Jun-4, Jun-12, Jun-20, Jun-28,
Jul-6, Jul-14, Jul-22, Jul-30,
Aug-7, Aug-15, Aug-23, Aug-31,
Sep-2, Sep-8, Sep-16, Sep-24,
Oct-2, Oct-10, Oct-18, Oct-26,
Nov-3, Nov-11, Nov-17, Nov-27,
Dec-5, Dec-13, Dec-21, Dec-29

Emotion:

Jan-3, Jan-11, Jan-19, Jan-27,
Feb-4, Feb-12, Feb-20, Feb-28,
Mar-15, Mar-23, Mar-31,
Apr-8, Apr-16, Apr-24,
May-2, May-10, May-18, May-26,
Jun-3, Jun-11, Jun-19, Jun-27,
Jul-5, Jul-12, Jul-21, Jul-29,
Aug-6, Aug-14, Aug-22, Aug-30,
Sep-7, Sep-15, Sep-23,
Oct-1, Oct-9, Oct-17, Oct-25,
Nov-2, Nov-10, Nov-18, Nov-26,
Dec-4, Dec-12, Dec-20, Dec-28

Mortality:

Jan-2, Jan-10, Jan-18, Jan-26,

Feb-3, Feb-11, Feb-19, Feb-27,
Mar-6, Mar-14, Mar-22, Mar-30,
Apr-7, Apr-15, Apr-23,
May-1, May-9, May-17, May-25,
Jun-2, Jun-10, Jun-13, Jun-18, Jun-26,
Jul-4, Jul-12, Jul-20, Jul-28,
Aug-5, Aug-13, Aug-21, Aug-29,
Sep-6, Sep-14, Sep-22, Sep-30,
Oct-8, Oct-16, Oct-24,
Nov-6, Nov-12, Nov-19, Nov-25,
Dec-3,Dec-19, Dec-22, Dec-27

Problem Solving:

Jan-7, Jan-15, Jan-23, Jan-31,
Feb-8, Feb-16, Feb-24,
Mar-3, Mar-11, Mar-19, Mar-27,
Apr-4, Apr-12, Apr-20, Apr-28,
May-6, May-14, May-22, May-30,
Jun-7, Jun-15, Jun-23,
Jul-1, Jul-9, Jul-17, Jul-25,
Aug-2, Aug-10, Aug-18, Aug-26,
Sep-3, Sep-11, Sep-19, Sep-27,
Oct-5, Oct-13, Oct-21, Oct-29,
Nov-7, Nov-14, Nov-22, Nov-30,
Dec-8, Dec-16, Dec-24

Resilience:

Jan-8, Jan-16, Jan-24,
Feb-1, Feb-9, Feb-17, Feb-25,
Mar-4, Mar-12, Mar-20, Mar-28,
Apr-5, Apr-13, Apr-21, Apr-29,

May-7, May-15, May-23, May-31,
Jun-8, Jun-16, Jun-24,
Jul-2, Jul-10, Jul-18, Jul-26,
Aug-3, Aug-11, Aug-19, Aug-27,
Sep-4, Sep-12, Sep-20, Sep-28,
Oct-6, Oct-14, Oct-22, Oct-30,
Nov-1, Nov-15, Nov-23,
Dec-1, Dec-9, Dec-17, Dec-25

Social Thought:

Jan-5, Jan-13, Jan-21, Jan-29,
 Feb-6, Feb-14, Feb-22,
 Mar-1, Mar-9, Mar-17, Mar-25,
 Apr-2, Apr-10, Apr-18, Apr-26,
 May-4, May-12, May-20, May-28,
 Jun-5, Jun-13, Jun-21, Jun-29,
 Jul-7, Jul-15, Jul-23, Jul-31,
 Aug-8, Aug-16, Aug-24,
 Sep-1, Sep-9, Sep-17, Sep-25,
 Oct-3, Oct-11, Oct-19, Oct-27,
 Nov-4, Nov-9, Nov-20, Nov-28,
 Dec-6, Dec-11, Dec-14, Dec-30

Did you love *Lap Around the Sun*? Then you should read *Joy in Alzheimer's*[1] by William Barron!

Experience the transformative power of this heart-wrenching true story, Joy in Alzheimer's. Witness how one woman's journey through dementia forever changed her and those around her. This book not only sheds light on the effects of Alzheimer's, but also offers valuable resources and information for those facing similar challenges.

- Learn how to navigate the early signs of Alzheimer's and receive a diagnosis with grace and strength.
- Discover the emotional toll that this disease takes on both the individual and their loved ones.
- Find comfort in the relatable and touching accounts of the author's personal experience.

---

1. https://books2read.com/u/mgxqyK

2. https://books2read.com/u/mgxqyK

- Gain a deeper understanding of Alzheimer's and its impact on the brain through informative research and references.

- Embrace the journey of acceptance and growth as you follow the story until its poignant end.

In Joy in Alzheimer's, you will find:

- A raw and honest depiction of the realities of Alzheimer's.

- A wealth of resources and information to help you and your loved ones cope with the challenges of this disease.

- Personal insights and heartfelt reflections from the author's own experience.

- A deeper understanding of the effects of Alzheimer's on the brain and how it can change a person.

- A message of hope and resilience in the face of adversity.

Read more at simplebender.com.

Also by William Barron

Joy in Alzheimer's
Lap Around the Sun

Watch for more at simplebender.com.

www.ingramcontent.com/pod-product-compliance
Lightning Source LLC
Chambersburg PA
CBHW020937180426
43194CB00038B/214